FACTS AND OBSERVATIONS
RELATIVE TO THE INFLUENCE
OF MANUFACTURES UPON HEALTH AND LIFE

The Development of Industrial Society Series

Daniel Noble

Facts and Observations
relative to the
INFLUENCE OF MANUFACTURES UPON HEALTH AND LIFE

IRISH UNIVERSITY PRESS
Shannon   Ireland

First edition London and Manchester 1843

This I U P reprint is a photolithographic facsimile of
the first edition and is unabridged, retaining the
original printer's imprint.

© *1971 Irish University Press Shannon Ireland*

All forms of micropublishing
© *Irish University Microforms Shannon Ireland*

ISBN 0 7165 1563 6

T M MacGlinchey Publisher

Irish University Press Shannon Ireland

PRINTED IN THE REPUBLIC OF IRELAND BY
ROBERT HOGG PRINTER TO IRISH UNIVERSITY PRESS

The Development of Industrial Society Series

This series comprises reprints of contemporary documents and commentaries on the social, political and economic upheavals in nineteenth-century England.

England, as the first industrial nation, was also the first country to experience the tremendous social and cultural impact consequent on the alienation of people in industrialized countries from their rural ancestry. The Industrial Revolution which had begun to intensify in the mid-eighteenth century, spread swiftly from England to Europe and America. Its effects have been far-reaching: the growth of cities with their urgent social and physical problems; greater social mobility; mass education; increasingly complex administration requirements in both local and central government; the growth of democracy and the development of new theories in economics; agricultural reform and the transformation of a way of life.

While it would be pretentious to claim for a series such as this an in-depth coverage of all these aspects of the new society, the works selected range in content from *The Hungry Forties* (1904), a collection of letters by ordinary working people describing their living conditions and the effects of mechanization on their day-to-day lives, to such analytical studies as Leone Levi's *History of British Commerce* (1880) and *Wages and Earnings of the Working Classes* (1885); M. T. Sadler's *The Law of Population* (1830); John Wade's radical documentation of government corruption, *The Extraordinary Black Book* (1831); C. Edward Lester's trenchant social investigation, *The Glory and Shame of England* (1866); and many other influential books and pamphlets.

The editor's intention has been to make available important contemporary accounts, studies and records, written or compiled by men and women of integrity and scholarship whose reactions to the growth of a new kind of society are valid touchstones for today's reader. Each title (and the particular edition used) has been chosen on a twofold basis (1) its intrinsic worth as a record or commentary, and (2) its contribution to the development of an industrial society. It is hoped that this collection will help to increase our understanding of a people and an epoch.

The Editor
Irish University Press

FACTS AND OBSERVATIONS

RELATIVE TO THE

INFLUENCE OF MANUFACTURES

UPON

HEALTH AND LIFE.

BY

DANIEL NOBLE,

MEMBER OF THE ROYAL COLLEGE OF SURGEONS IN LONDON,
OF THE LITERARY AND PHILOSOPHICAL SOCIETY
OF MANCHESTER, ETC. ETC.

LONDON:

JOHN CHURCHILL, PRINCES STREET, SOHO.

MANCHESTER: SIMMS AND DINHAM.   LEEDS: SLOCOMBE AND SIMMS.

MDCCCXLIII.

C. AND J. ADLARD, PRINTERS, BARTHOLOMEW CLOSE

PREFACE.

THE British and Foreign Medical Review, for April of the present year, opens with an article, from the pen of the present writer, on the influence of manufactures upon health; which article constitutes the basis of the present production. The Author's special researches upon the subject in question were undertaken at the instance of DR. FORBES, the learned Editor of the above-named periodical, without there being any intention, at the time, of rendering the results matter for separate publication. It has been at the advice and solicitation of friends, in whose judgment the Author confides, that he has been induced to issue the following pages: and it is with extreme diffidence that he now submits them to the general reader.

MANCHESTER; *July*, 1843.

CONTENTS.

PAGE

Section I.

Previous Views and Researches   -   -   -   1

Section II.

General Facts of the Case   -   -   -   -   31

Section III.

Alleged Particular Evils   - -   -   -   56

INFLUENCE OF MANUFACTURES

UPON

HEALTH AND LIFE.

SECTION I.

PREVIOUS VIEWS AND RESEARCHES.

THERE are few questions whose complete and satisfactory solution furnishes matter of higher importance,
yet points of greater difficulty, than the one relating to
the influence of employments upon health and life. This
must be apparent to all who have watched the issue of
the various attempts which have been made to elucidate
the subject within a comparatively recent period. And,
indeed, when it is considered how thoroughly charac-
teristic of our present advanced state of civilization is
the extraordinary progression of manufactures and the
mechanical arts, and how intimately the condition of
these bears upon most things affecting the welfare of
humanity, it is little to be wondered at, that their moral,
social, and sanatory effects should have constituted the
theme of reiterated researches—researches, however,
which in many instances have led to no very satisfactory
results ; for, like every other subject identified or intimately mixed up with human interests and feelings,
this one has shown itself to be the fertile occasion of

statements and opinions of the most opposite and conflicting nature.

One class of inquirers guided more, probably, by over-
wrought sentiments of humanity than by unbiassed judgment, have looked upon the discovery of the steam-engine
and its application to the increase of our manufactures
as little less than an unmitigated injury done to the bulk
of society, accumulating the fruits of labour within
the possession of a small number of capitalists, to the
utter destruction of all health and comfort on the part
of the actual producers of wealth; whilst an opposite
class—regarding the whole matter from another point
of view, and more under the influence of a cool and
calculating (probably selfish) political economy—have
maintained that the extension of arts and manufactures
in modern times has been an unalloyed benefit to the
world, and one carrying with it the least possible amount
of disadvantage to the masses engaged therein. Others
again—estimating the subject less controlled by feeling,
and more in the spirit of accurate and unprejudiced inquiry—have come to intermediate conclusions, believing
that more or less of evil has resulted to great numbers,
coincidently with very great benefits to mankind as a
whole.

It were indeed a strange proposition to maintain that
an extension and enlargement of human capability
should operate, inevitably, to the prejudice of the race;
and, whatever be the evils that do actually accompany
a high degree of civilization, they ought surely to be
regarded, not as something inseparable from and in-
herent in such a state of things, but as the temporary
result of that human imperfection which allows man to
become enlightened, not in all things at once, but only

progressively. (The immense development of mechanical skill within the last half century, the great consequent extension of manufactures, and increase in the number, size, and density of our modern towns, furnish an excellent illustration of that puzzling combination of good and evil which leads some minds absolutely to condemn all human improvement in this direction, and to maintain the paradox that the condition of man is deteriorated by the steady increase of his natural powers. Would not a sound wisdom, however, apply itself to discover by cautious analysis the real source of the attendant evil, and to see if its rectification could not be accomplished without the necessity of acting upon so contradictory a doctrine as would seem to be involved in the position just referred to?

The extent to which the evil in question bears upon the sanatory condition of our manufacturing population forms, cerainly, no unimportant part of any investigation undertaken with the above object; and as there attaches to the question just now, from a variety of circumstances, an unusual amount of interest, I propose in the following pages to furnish to the reader the results to which I have been led by a careful examination of the various sources of information which, in the present state of our knowledge, seem calculated to elucidate the inquiry. Much having been said, and written, and adduced in evidence, intended to support every view of the case, and the whole matter being one of so extensive and multifarious and complex a character, I am well aware that any attempt to shed new light upon the question, within the compass of a few brief pages, must prove both imperfect and unsatisfactory; nevertheless, from its great importance at the present moment, I am induced to enter upon the task, in the confidence that I may, at least approximatively, determine some of the positive facts and conclusions made out in the investigation.

It is known to all persons interested in this subject, that at various times within the present century, the sanatory influence of the cotton manufacture has attracted a more than usual share of attention. This is in great part attributable, no doubt, to its recent most extraordinary rate of increase, and to the revolution it has wrought in the general condition of those parts of the country wherein it is extensively prevalent. It has been found that immense aggregations of individuals have arisen, within a very few years, in districts previously almost rural; and that the means of subsistence afforded to such dense masses of human beings has flowed mainly from the existence of what is popularly called the "factory system." This system, it has been the custom to describe, as one leading to the crowding together, in heated apartments, of persons of all ages and sexes, who have little or no opportunity either for rest, fresh air, or healthful recreation. Such a state of things has naturally enough been stigmatised as the fell destroyer of youth, and as the remote origin of almost every ailment that may in after life afflict its surviving victims. The prevalence of these notions having powerfully excited the sympathy of many benevolent persons, this matter has often been made the subject of detailed inquiry, by parliamentary committees, special commissions, and also by private individuals; and a vast amount of information, bearing upon the whole question, has in consequence been obtained.

The investigation whose results seem most to have

influenced both the legislature and the country is the one which was prosecuted under Mr. Sadler's auspices by a committee of the House of Commons about the year 1832. On account of the great impression which the published evidence, obtained upon this occasion, produced at the time; and, more particularly, as its effects upon public opinion are as yet far from being extinguished; I think it right here to adduce the substance of the *medical* testimony, with the view of considering and examining to what extent a more precise and enlarged acquaintance with the real facts of the case will confirm, or otherwise, the statements and opinions advanced upon this occasion.

The factory system, it will then be found by referring to the proper parliamentary documents, was almost unanimously condemned and denounced as the abundant source of pallid looks, stunted growth, personal deformity, and chronic disease of various kinds. One of the first medical witnesses examined before Mr. Sadler's committee was Dr. Thomas Young, of Bolton, to whose evidence much value must have been attached, from the circumstance of his residence and practice being in the midst of the cotton manufacture. This gentleman, on being asked respecting his " opinions as to the medical effects produced by the hours of labour, deduced as well from the principles of his profession, as from actual experience," replies as follows:—" The first effects appear to be upon the digestion, the appetite suffers, the digestion is impaired, and consequent emaciation and debility are induced. Scrofulous diseases are common; I am not aware that this disease would be produced in a sound child born of healthy parents, but if a predisposition to scrofula existed in the constitution,

the disease (which might otherwise probably have re-
mained dormant in the system) is likely to be called into
action." Next, it was demanded of this witness,
—"Have you observed whether pulmonary complaints
are the frequent result of such labour ?" It is replied,
"They are; for example, consumption and asthma; the
latter, however, I have more frequently observed in
adults than in children." Again,—"but so as clearly
to be traceable, in your judgment, to the particular
nature of the employment to which reference is made ?"
—"Certainly; to the transition from excessive heat to
cold, and the inhalation of dust and cotton-flue." The
same witness, after dwelling at some length upon the
tendency of factory labour to induce scrofulous deformity and disease generally, sums up by observing that
"he could not doubt that factory labour tended to
shorten life, inasmuch as it tended to produce disease."
It would thus be concluded, if Dr. Young must receive
credit as an accurate and impartial observer, that chronic
disease, mainly of a scrofulous character, was developed
and fostered by the extension of the cotton manufacture.

Most of the medical witnesses, however, who were examined before Mr. Sadler's committee, were metropolitan
practitioners, whose general reputation suggested them
to the committee as suitable persons to give information
upon the physiological effects of certain kinds of occupation. The working of the factory system, however,
was for the most part known to them only through the
descriptions which were afforded, and hence the value
of their evidence sustains considerable diminution,
although it is that which seems most to have influenced
both the legislature and public opinion. There was yet
one metropolitan witness, Mr. Malyn, whose early days,

it appears, had been spent in Manchester, the capital of the cotton manufacture; and this gentleman furnishes the following testimony, relative to the sanatory condition of the operative classes in this town: "As a practitioner, and as an observer of facts, I can affirm that there exists a marked difference between the operatives of the metropolis and those whose condition you are now investigating. As a physiologist, and as such, reasoning on those facts, I have been led to connect that difference with the nature and the duration of their employment." When asked,—" Is not that disorder (scrofula) peculiarly prevalent in Manchester?" he replies,—" It is to a great degree; nor have I, in the observations I have made elsewhere, ever seen it so common as it is in that town. Speaking from general recollection, I should say, I have not witnessed, since my departure from that place, one tenth of what I observed there; although I have ever made it a rule (when otherwise unoccupied) to continue my researches among the poor." All this is startling, certainly; how far these vague statements "from general recollection" have any probable foundation in fact, the reader may be in some condition to judge, on arriving at the close of the present publication.

Dr. Blundell, a London physician of high physiological repute, is appealed to by the committee for his views as to the effects upon individuals, and especially children, to be looked for from pursuing the kind of occupation described to him by the examinant, as " the labour in question, continued for the length of time described, (thirteen, fourteen, fifteen, and even eighteen or nineteen hours a day;) without sufficient and often without any intervals, even for meals, generally pursued

in an erect, or at least a constrained position, and in a
foul and polluted atmosphere, frequently heated to a
very high temperature, and many times continued far
into or during the whole of the night." The effects
expected by the witness under such circumstances are
"dyspeptic symptoms, and all their consequences;
nervous diseases in greater or less degree; and, as the
result of both, stunted growth; languors; lassitude;
general debility; and a recourse to sensual stimulants,
in order to rid the mind of its distressing feelings." The
examinant, in the progress of Dr. Blundell's evidence,
states that "an official paper has been ordered by and
delivered to this committee, which shows the great
waste of human life, especially at its earliest stages, in
the manufacturing or factory districts, as compared with
the mortality at corresponding periods of life in other
towns and places." This latter statement is most remarkable, not on account of its truth, but because it
furnishes an excellent illustration of the way in which
wholesale deductions, resting upon most imperfect data,
were hazarded during this parliamentary investigation.
This will be apparent when, in the progress of these
pages, the subject shall have been authoritatively decided by an appeal to the documents of the Registrar-
general,—documents which furnish much more complete
and accurate materials respecting all such matters, than
any which were to be obtained anterior to, or during
the proceedings instituted by Mr. Sadler.

Dr. Hodgkin, another metropolitan physician of just
and merited celebrity, is questioned respecting his an-
ticipations as to the probable effects of the factory
system, judging of this latter according to the descriptions which had been afforded. Results of a most

disastrous character are of course inferred. "Great depression of the general health, diminutive stature, varicose ulceration of the lower extremities, scrofulous deformity, premature attainment of puberty leading to most immoral consequences;" and the climax is attained by the conclusion, that "where the system prevails extensively a considerable abridgment of human life must be the obvious consequence."

Mr. John Morgan, surgeon to Guy's Hospital, is subjected to an examination somewhat in the same strain, furnishing his answers apparently with equal satisfaction to the committee. I shall here adduce one observation made by this gentleman; it is too choice to be passed over without notice. He says, " the employment of a chimney-sweeper I should consider, *perhaps,* more injurious than *even* these manufactories."

Amongst the medical witnesses giving evidence before this committee, the late Sir Anthony Carlisle occupies a prominent position. Although examined at considerable length, there is little in his evidence differing from or in addition to that afforded by the others whose testimony I have just noticed. Some observations, however, made on the occasion by this witness I shall here extract, as containing, I apprehend, matter that is somewhat questionable. In discussing the probable effects of the factory system much in the same style as the foregoing witnesses, he avers, constructively at least, that its direct tendency is to check population by rendering marriages less fruitful. He volunteers also the following remarkable statement which, however, does not refer to the destructive effects of manufactures, though furnished in indirect confirmation of the above position: "I would offer to the committee," says he, "a matter in my own experience; the city of London would not maintain its population for fifty years, if it was not refreshed by accessions from the country. I have had the curiosity to see if I could find a person of the fourth generation, by both the father and mother's side in the city of London, and I have never been able to find such a person."

The statement on the part of an examining member of the committee respecting the unusual rate of mortality in the districts where the cotton manufacture prevails, is repeated in yet stronger terms during the examination of the late Sir W. Blizard, to whom it is said,—"wherever this (the factory) system prevails it is accompanied by an extraordinary degree of mortality, especially in the earlier periods of life; taking the view you have done of the pernicious effects of labour so long pursued, and under the circumstances explained, you would be prepared for that result, namely, a greatly increased degree of mortality?" To this, the witness replies: "I do not know the fact; but, *a priori*, I should have no doubt of it, not the shadow of one." It is also the recorded opinion of Sir William that factory labour, as described, must lead to the premature attainment of womanhood; and, in this view, he is corroborated by other medical witnesses, and, as before stated, in very strong terms by Dr. Hodgkin.

It is demanded of Dr. Elliotson, by the committee, what he conceives would be likely to result from such a system of labour; and to this he promptly replies, "scrofulous diseases of every description, consumption, and deformities."

In these extracts from the report of Mr. Sadler's committee, I cannot omit to notice the very decisive character of the evidence of that accomplished surgeon, Mr. Green, of St. Thomas's Hospital, who, after stating that he cannot pretend to any practical experience in these matters, says, "I may yet be able to contribute some information that my professional duties have enabled me to acquire, in aid of your benevolent purpose of duly limiting the hours of infantile and early labour." Upon this, we have a most able and lucid exposition of the causes that excite and predispose to scrofulous disease, with the order in which its various forms are commonly developed, and the whole wound up with the following:—" And lastly, the lungs become the seat of this destructive disease in the form of that incurable complaint of our climate, pulmonary consumption." All this is placed in direct relation to the factory system by the mode in which the answers succeed the questions, and Mr. Green "fears that this country will have much to answer for, in permitting the growth of that system of employing children in factories, which tends directly to the creation of all those circumstances which inevitably lead to disease."

Before closing with the results of this parliamentary investigation I shall extract one or two of the more striking passages occurring in the evidence of Dr. J. R. Farre. "In English factories," he says, "everything which is valuable in manhood is sacrificed to an inferior advantage in childhood. You purchase your advantage at the price of infanticide; the profit thus gained is death to the child. Looking to its effects, I should suppose it was a system directly intended to diminish population." To the above strong expressions, applied to the factory system, I subjoin the following observations, having a more extended relation: "I call the British system a forcing system, which departs from the truth of nature and the revealed will of God. I have no hesitation in affirming that there is not a due regard to the preservation of life, either in the British system of education or of labour generally, both as regards the child and the adult; and what I say of the adult applies still more strongly to the child."

The above quotations furnish the main substance of the testimony afforded by the medical witnesses upon the occasion referred to; and, assuredly, if the conclusions to which the whole points have any material foundation in fact, it is difficult to say what national advantages ought not to be sacrificed rather than that a system so destructive to humanity, both morally and physically speaking, should be allowed to go on without the application of some grave check. In reviewing, however, the whole of the circumstances connected with the above evidence, it becomes clear that considerable one-sidedness is mixed up with the mode in which the testimony is obtained. The replies of the medical witnesses are almost invariably to leading questions; and when they refer to factory labour in express terms, it is to the labour as described to them in the exaggerated phraseology of the examining members of the committee, who, but too often, in their way of conducting the investigation, remind one of the proceeding of the advocate in making out a case, rather than of that of the impartial inquirer after the truth. It is strikingly confirmatory of this view of the case, that, out of eighteen medical witnesses examined almost successively, sixteen were metropolitan and two only from the manufacturing districts; and that one of these two, Mr. Thackrah of Leeds, was a practitioner resident, not in the districts of the cotton, but of the woollen manufactures. Indeed, in going through this evidence, little is discovered practically, beyond a series of judicious observations upon hygiène, accompanied with strictures upon the way in which its laws are presumed to be infringed by the proprietors of cotton mills.

I have said that considerable one-sidedness attaches to the character of the medical evidence, and that the severity and hardship of factory labour are described in obviously exaggerated phraseology; this will be apparent from a review of some of the more important facts and circumstances developed, respecting this matter, in the progress of subsequent inquiries.

Very shortly after this parliamentary committee had closed its labours, in the year 1833, it was thought desirable to obtain a more precise and definite acquaintance with the entire facts of the case than the labours of Mr. Sadler and his associates were considered to lead to. Accordingly, certain commissioners, including Sir David Barry, Dr. London, and Dr. Bissett Hawkins, were deputed by government to collect, upon the spot, all available materials for basing just conclusions upon ; and, with this design, the commissioners distributed themselves, and obtained a vast amount of information concerning both the moral, social, and sanatory influence of manufactures. Portions of the reports, relating to the subject of these pages, I proceed to adduce, from which it will be obvious that I have done Mr. Sadler's committee no injustice by the mode in which I have characterized its proceedings. The subjoined accounts have reference to the condition of the manufacturing operatives in Dumfermline, Scotland, and are taken from the second report of the Factory Commission :

" Sir David Barry, whose medical evidence on this subject is peculiarly valuable, because it is in every instance the result of personal inspection and strict examination, reports as follows :

" The health of the operatives in general appears excellent ; some few look rather delicate, but seem to work cheerfully. The appearance of by far the greater number was healthful, robust, fully grown for age ; did not see even one case of distortion or narrow pelvis. Many of the girls were beautifully formed, who had been from ten years to maturity in the mill. . . . . He (Dr. Stephenson) states that parents send their least promising offspring to the mill, and their most robust to trades and agriculture. With regard to the physical appearance of the young persons, I went round the village whilst they were at dinner, and saw no squalid, emaciated, nor stunted individuals. . . . . This day examined carefully and individually one hundred and eleven girls of the classes stated, with a view to find, if possible, a case in which the plantar arch had been broken down by continual standing, as is stated in the evidence lately printed to occur sometimes in factory workers. Found many beautifully formed feet in those who had worked the longest."

The following extract refers to the state of things in Manchester, and is from Dr. B. Hawkins's contribution to the report :

" I believe that most travellers are struck by the lowness of stature, the leanness, and the paleness which present themselves so commonly to the eye at Manchester, and above all among the factory classes. I have never been in any town in Great Britain nor in Europe in which degeneracy of form and colour from the national standard has been so obvious.

" It is impossible not to notice the total absence of public gardens, parks, and walks at Manchester; it is scarcely in the power of the factory worker to taste the breath of nature or to look upon its verdure, and this defect is a strong impediment to convalescence from disease, which is usually tedious and difficult at Manchester."

In the progress of Dr. Hawkins's researches, prosecuted in many cases conjointly with his colleagues, certain statements are made which tend to elucidate the actual value of some of the facts obtained during this inquiry. Thus, in the examination of Samuel Holt, Joseph Gaskill, and John Rowbotham, overlookers in Messrs. Birley's mill, the following occurs:

" Q. Have you observed any bad effects on the health of your children produced by their employment in factories, and particularly in the card-room?

"(Mr. Rowbotham.) None whatever; I think they are as healthy as they would have been in any employment that I know of.

" Q. Is it the case that children who, from scrofula or weakness, or ill health of some kind, are unfitted for many of the usual occupations at which children are placed, are fit for some descriptions of factory-work?

" (All.) This is the case.

"(Mr. Gaskill.) Children who are naturally deformed, others who are weak in their limbs, others who have weakly health, are in Mr. Birley's employ, and I do not see what they could do, or what they are fit for, except some work in factories."

These statements respecting the adaptation of children of delicate or scrofulous constitution for mill-work only, and their destination for the same on that account, cor-

respond with the information before adduced, which
Sir David Barry obtained in another part of the kingdom.   If strictly true, they may probably shed some
light upon the circumstances mentioned below, sup-
posing the arrangement of them to have been formed
impartially.

I again extract from Dr. Hawkins's report.

" In order to ascertain the state of health of the
youthful factory classes, compared with youth in other
conditions, I made a careful examination of the Bennett-
street Sunday-school at Manchester, in which abundance
of all trades exists.   I accordingly took an account of
350 of both sexes not engaged in factories, and of 350
of both sexes engaged in factories.   Of the former,
several remain at home and do nothing; some are in
service, some are dress-makers, some engaged in warehouses and in shops.   Their age varied from nine years
to twenty for the most part.

> *Of* 350 *not in Factories:*
>> 21 had bad health.
>> 88 had middling health.
>> 241 had good health.
>
> *But of* 350 *in Factories.*
>> 73 had bad health.
>> 134 had middling health.
>> 143 had good health.

"Again at the St. Augustine's Sunday-school at
Manchester, I compared fifty boys engaged in factories
with fifty others, some of whom lived at home doing
nothing, while others were engaged in shops and in
various trades.

Of the 50 *not in Factories,*
   1 had bad health,
   18 had middling health.
   31 had good health.
But of the 50 *in Factories,*
   13 had bad health.
   19 had middling health.
   18 had good health.

" It will be seen that the advantage of health is at least double at these institutions on the side of those young people who are not engaged in factories."

Notwithstanding the evidence bearing upon this matter, supplied to the factory commissioners by certain persons in the employment of Mr. Birley, the above figures tell *primá facie* very decisively against what is called the factory system ; but they do not correspond with other facts selected, in the judgment of the present writer, upon a principle less likely to lead to erroneous conclusions.   These other facts I shall bring forward in the sequel, and at the same time state certain reasons which lead me to the belief that a fallacy is involved in the above proceeding of Dr. Hawkins, although it is one which, at first sight, seems so entirely unexceptionable.

The results obtained by the factory commissioners upon this occasion, relative to the sanatory condition of persons engaged in manufactures, were of very diversified character, varying for the most part according to the density of the population in particular localites; and as the evidence generally was collected apparently in a fair and unbiassed manner, and in a great measure from actual observation, the conclusions carry with them, necessarily, far greater weight than do those published by the parliamentary committee.

Some very interesting information respecting the whole subject of manufacturing industry was supplied, in the year 1835, by Dr. Ure, in his ‘Philosophy of Manufactures,’ a work which exhibits proof of the greatest attention and labour having been bestowed upon the investigation. Some of the author's statements are both curious and important, especially when placed in contrast with the direful details furnished by Mr. Sadler's witnesses. As Dr. Ure's inquiries took place at a period of high manufacturing prosperity, in the well-remembered years 1834-5, it is very natural that an undue bias, in the favorable direction, should have arisen; and, certainly, Dr. Ure's book manifests no little exaggeration and partiality in his selection of illustrations. Nevertheless, the facts and conclusions possess considerable value from the circumstance of their having been obtained upon the spot; Dr. Ure having, as is well known to many, resided for some time in Manchester and the neighbourhood, whilst accumulating his materials.

I have said, in commenting upon the proceedings of the factory committee, that the hardship and severity of factory labour were described to the medical witnesses in obviously exaggerated phraseology; and this will be apparent from the statements of Dr. Ure, who informs us that, instead of the labour being pursued almost through the entire night, it is but rarely carried beyond twelve hours out of the twenty-four, and that night-work is scouted by all respectable mill-owners, as being equally unprofitable and demoralizing. Much had been said respecting the atmosphere of cotton-mills being

" foul and polluted;" Dr. Ure, however, says that, so far is this from being the case, there exists in many instances a system of ventilation of very great superiority, as will appear from the following passage, occurring at page 380, of the 'Philosophy of Manufactures :'

" The factory plan is to extract the foul air, in measurable volumes, by mechanical means of the simplest but most unfailing kind, especially by eccentric fans made to revolve with the rapidity of nearly 100 feet per second, and thereby to ensure a constant renewal of the atmosphere in any range of apartments, however large or closely pent they may be."

Respecting the temperature of cotton-mills, a branch of the subject concerning which very exaggerated statements had gone abroad, Dr. Ure observes at page 400 :

" In Manchester, whenever the temperature of the external air is genial, no artificial heat is used in the fine-spinning mills, which never require a heat above 75° Fahr., as several respectable witnesses prove on oath."

With regard to that " crowding together of individuals" in the apartments of cotton-mills, upon which so much stress had been laid, " it is utterly impossible," says Dr. Ure, like one describing what he had actually seen, " from the nature of the machinery. The mules, in their advancing and retreating locomotion, must have five or six times the space to work in that the actual bulk of the mechanism requires. Now, nine tenths of the children are employed tending these open-spaced mules. Any one who has once visited a cotton-spinning room must be aware of the impossibility of unduly crowding human beings in a mule apartment. Nor are any of the other rooms crowded with workers, for this plain reason, that no useful purpose could thence result to the manufacturer."

The substantial accuracy of the above description of factory labour will at once be recognized by all having positive and direct acquaintance with the subject. I shall now present to the reader some of the results respecting the health of the operatives, to which Dr. Ure was led by his researches. On regarding the morbid effects attributed by large numbers to the prevalence of the factory system, diseases, of the character and class ordinarily comprehended in the term " scrofula," seem to constitute the sum of the alleged consequences; thus, the vicious digestion, the nervous debility, and glandular disease ; the stunted growth, osseous deformity, and pulmonary consumption; all these, as forming its special manifestations, were the results anticipated by medical *reasoners ;* let us then see whether the testimony of medical *observers* deposes, with anything like uniformity, to the justness of such an inference, Upon this subject, Dr. Ure rushes to conclusions at utter variance with all the notions that had previously been entertained. It may be gathered both from the tenor of his own remarks, and the character of the references which he approvingly makes, that, in his estimation, not only is the factory system *not* prejudicial to health, or tending to the development of scrofulous disease, but, on the contrary, actually preservative of the former, and to some extent curative of the latter. Agricultural employment, which all the world had ordinarily thought to be more salubrious than town pursuits, ranks only secondarily in a sanatory point of view. A communication, formerly made to the factory commissioners by the late Dr. Carbutt of this town, is inserted by Dr. Ure in his work, at page 376; and in this communication the following occurs: "The fact is, that scrofula is almost unknown in cotton factories, although the climate of this town and neighbourhood is particularly cold and humid. In a very extensive examination, which I and some other medical men made a few years ago, we found to our surprise that the cotton factories, instead of producing scrofula, are, in some sort, a kind of means of cure. . . . . . In one factory, examined by Dr. Holme, and Mr. Scott, surgeon to the carabineers, of 401 persons employed, eight persons only were affected with scrofula, with no case of distortion of the spine or limbs. . . . . In addition to the above facts, I may mention that, during the sixteen years I have had the honour of being physician to the Manchester Royal Infirmary, I have nearly invariably, at the consultations previously to operation, to which the physicians are summoned as well as the surgeon, been in the habit of putting to the patient the question, 'What trade are you of?' especially when the case was that of distorted limb or joint. To which question, the answer has almost never been, 'Work in a cotton factory,' but almost constantly, 'A hand-loom weaver;' or, 'A hatter,' or some other trade."

The above statements, though exaggerated without doubt, possess nevertheless very considerable interest. They proceeded from a practical physician, resident in the metropolis of the factory district, with excellent opportunities for arriving at a knowledge of the true facts of the case, and they cannot but carry with them some weight and importance. However, I go on to notice the further evidence collected by Dr. Ure in support of his views regarding the influence of cotton-mills

on health.   The circumstance related below, in the
before-mentioned work, is remarkable, but reference is
not made to the authority upon which the statement
rests :

" During the prevalence of the cholera at Stockport,
it was observed that the mill-workers enjoyed a remarkable immunity from the attack; an immunity due to the
warm air which surrounded them while at work, and to
the comforts of their homes.   The cholera patients in
that town were almost all females employed in private
dwellings."

The following from Dr. Ure, if literally true, constitutes a very singular fact :

" Not one of Messrs. Strutt's work-people at Belper
was attacked with cholera, while the neighbouring
handicraft people and farmers were falling victims to
this pestilence."

Dr. Ure has introduced into his book a very valuable
document, in relation to this question, in the form of a
report made some years ago by Mr. Harrison, the in-
specting-surgeon appointed for the mills of Preston and
its vicinity, within the limits of whose jurisdiction it
seems that there were 1656 individuals employed in
mills under eighteen years of age, of whom 952 were
employed in spinning-rooms, 468 in carding-rooms,
128 at power-looms, and 108 in winding, skewering
cops, &c.   Mr. Harrison reports as under:

" I have made very particular inquiries respecting the
health of every child whom I have examined, and I
find that the average annual sickness of each child is
not more than four days; at least, that not more than
four days on an average are lost by each child in a
year in consequence of sickness.   This includes disorders

of every kind, for the most part induced by causes wholly unconnected with factory labour. I have been not a little surprised to find so little sickness which can fairly be attributed to mill-work. I have met with very few children who have suffered from injuries occasioned by machinery; and the protection, especially in new factories, is now so complete that accidents will, I doubt not, speedily become rare. I have not met with a single instance, out of the 1656 children whom I have examined, of deformity that is referrible to factory labour. It must be admitted that factory children do not present the same blooming robust appearance as is witnessed among children who labour in the open air, but I question if they are not more exempt from acute diseases, and do not, on the whole, suffer less sickness than those who are regarded as having more healthy employments. The average age at which the children of this district enter the factories is ten years and two months; and the average age of all the young persons together is fourteen years."

Dr. Ure, in further support of his views regarding the salubrious influence of the factory system, adduces a variety of other testimony; and, that too, from persons whose opportunities must have made them practically acquainted with the subject. And, truly, when all this is placed in juxta-position with the evidence which I have noticed of a totally opposite character, it furnishes materials for a judgment but little complimentary either to medical reasoning or to medical observation. On the one hand, we have our deepest sympathies excited in commiseration of the unfortunate victims of manufacturing avarice; and, on the other, we are gladdened to the heart that modern advance in civilization, with its

mechanical improvements and increased means of production, has, whilst enriching the capitalist, trebled and
quadrupled the health, and the happiness, and the bodily
comforts of the most helpless of our fellow-creatures?
What must we conclude amidst such conflicting testimony? I shall postpone the attempt to determine, and
resume the review of what has already been done in
the progress of this investigation.

The state of the working classes has attracted, of late
years, in France, as well as in our own country, considerable attention; and the influence of manufactures
upon the sanatory condition of the persons who are
engaged in them has received its due share of regard.
The celebrated French statistician, Dr. Villermé, has
recently presented to the world certain results relative
to the moral and physical conditions of the operatives
employed in the manufacture of cotton, of wool, and of
silk, in a work undertaken by order of the Parisian
Academy of Moral and Political Science, and published
in the year 1840.* The following extracts from the
author's preface will explain the way in which the
inquiry arose, and, at the same time, furnish a kind of
guarantee for the accuracy of his observations, as
showing the scrupulous exactness with which he seems
to have prosecuted his labours :

"The Academy of Moral and Political Sciences com-
missioned M. Benoiston de Chateauneuf and myself to
make, in the departments of France, certain researches
in political economy and statistical science, the object of

* Tableau de l'Etat Physique et Moral des Ouvriers employés dans
les manufactures de Coton, de Laine, et de Soie. Ouvrage entrepris
par ordre de l'Académie des Sciences Morales et Politiques. Par
M. le Dr. Villermé.

which was to ascertain, as exactly as possible, the physical and moral condition of the working classes . . . .
For the purpose of rendering our mission more useful,
M. Benoiston de Chateauneuf and myself separated.
Whilst my associate traversed the centre of France and
the sea-coasts, I visited the departments where the
cotton, woollen, and silk manufactures chiefly engage
the workpeople. I shall premise, however, by stating
the mode in which I proceeded with my researches.
It was necessary for me to examine the effects of a work
upon those whom it employs, to interrogate misery
without humiliating it, and to observe misconduct without irritating it. This task was difficult. Well! I love
to say it, everywhere magistrates, physicians, manufacturers, mere workmen were anxious to second me.
By their aid, I have been enabled to see, to hear, and
to become acquainted with everything. They have
furnished me with information, as if in emulation of
one another. Some I got by direct inquiry, some I obtained unawares. And such is the care which I was
anxious to apply to this investigation, that I have followed the workman from his workshop to his dwelling.
I have entered there with him, I have studied him in
the bosom of his family; I have assisted at his meals.
I have done more; I had seen him in his toils and in
his household, I have wished to see him in his pleasures,
to observe him in his parties. There, listening to his
conversation, occasionally mingling therein, I have been,
unconsciously to himself, the confidant of his joys and
his sorrows, of his regrets and his hopes, the witness of
his vices and his virtues."

Such is the spirit with which Dr. Villermé set out in
the investigation; and, after the protestation of a pro-

cedure so truly philosophical, a very high interest and
consideration must attach to any testimony upon the
present subject which emanates from such a source.   I
shall here endeavour to comprise, within a brief compass, the substance of what is advanced regarding the
influence of the cotton manufacture upon the health of
its votaries.

He observes that, in the course of his various researches, he had heard much concerning the insalubrity
of this branch of industry.   After noticing the charge
of insufficient ventilation as a cause of disease, he pro-
ceeds to give the result of his own investigations upon
this point.   He, accordingly, furnishes an account of
the precise measures of the various work-rooms, with
the mode in which the air is renewed, and the number
which they inclose when in full operation; the conclusion is, that the great bulk of those employed in the
cotton-mills have a better supply at their work than at
their homes, and better also than great numbers of
other classes of workpeople.   In this branch of manufactures, however, there is, he says, one class of workpeople worse situated in a sanatory point of view than
the rest; he alludes to the *batters of cotton*, whose
occupation necessitates the inhalation of much dust and
flue ; this class, he states to include very small numbers,
and to be found only in the mills for fine spinning.
M. Villermé states that he discovered an entire accordance of opinion respecting the injurious influence of the
dusty atmosphere, on the part alike of workpeople, of
overlookers and managers, of the masters themselves,
and also of medical men.   Indeed, he says that the un-
healthful influence of cotton batting, whether done by
the hand or by machinery, is so generally admitted,

that workpeople, engaged therein, relieve one another like soldiers called to mount guard. He observes that, whether it be the dust contained in the raw cotton apart from the cotton flue, or this latter itself, which ruins the health of those engaged in the process, the decay of their health is ever certain, and an established fact; that they complain of dryness in the mouth, in the throat, and are seized sooner or later with a cough gradually increasing in severity.) "Nevertheless," he says, "I have met in the batting-rooms some men in good health who told me that they had worked there uninterruptedly for many years." The cough is the first symptom of a slow and formidable disease of the chest, which is always relieved on abandoning the work, and altogether cured at its commencement, if the employment be not resumed. The disease, in the process of its development, assumes all the characteristics of consumption, and the medical men, resident in the manufacturing districts, call it ' *cotton-consumption*,' (phthisie cotonneuse,) and some ' *cotton inflammation of the lungs*.' M. Villermé states that numbers from this cause die in the hospitals, but he could not ascertain in what proportion. Formerly, cotton-batting was invariably attended with all these inconveniences, but recent improvements in machinery, the author says, have remedied them in great measure; and the numbers subject to this hurtful agency have now become exceedingly limited. The carding of cotton which leads, to some extent, to an inspiration of a dusty atmosphere, is attended, he observes, with a like insalubrity, though in a much less degree. In all the subsequent processes, however, no inconvenience of this kind results.

M. Villermé notices in detail the supposed effects

upon the health of the elevated temperature required in certain factory processes.   For carding, he says that a heat of from 59° to 61° Fahr. is all that is needed ; for spinning, however, a higher temperature is required, a temperature rising in proportion to the fineness of the threads in course of fabrication, and varying accordingly from 64° to 104° Fahr. ; the extreme degree, however, is only demanded in comparatively few instances.   It seems that, according to the inquiries made, the results of the excessive heat could not be uniformly ascertained, as sometimes he was told that no other unpleasantness followed than a sort of erysipelatous inflammation about the bend of the thigh, especially in the case of fat persons, and that this necessitated them occasionally to relinquish their work for a short time only ; others stated that many work-people were in consequence obliged to abandon the fine-spinning work altogether ; and again it was said, that none but the young could endure the high temperature.   M. Villermé was also informed by many medical men, that an unusual number of those so employed were attacked with colds and severe inflammation of the chest, as a consequence of the sudden chilling to which they were exposed.   In other instances, however, where the excessive heat is not needed, the work-rooms maintain, especially during winter, a much more agreeable temperature than the operatives enjoy at their own houses.   The influence of the monotony and tediousness of factory labour in the production of pale looks and general languor of the system is slightly glanced at.

The above comprises the substance of M. Villermé's information respecting the health of the operatives engaged in the cotton manufacture, as obtained in his recent researches.   I shall have occasion again to refer

to the views and statements of this distinguished statistician, when attempting to deduce the positive conclusions to which, in the opinion of the present writer, the
just value of the premises ought to lead.

During the last summer, about the period of the
British Association's meeting in Manchester, Dr. Cooke
Taylor, the well-known author of the ' Natural History
of Civilization,' interested himself in the study of the
influence of the factory system upon the moral and
physical comforts of the population whom it mainly
supports.   His views regarding these matters are em-
bodied in a small volume, addressed, in the form of
letters, to the Archbishop of Dublin, and constituting a
series of reminiscences and records of a tour in the
manufacturing districts of Lancashire.   From Dr. Taylor's
somewhat rapid and necessarily superficial survey of the
various matters upon which he expatiates, little can be
taken that possesses the character of very strong evidence.   I refer to his work because it forms somewhere
about the last link in this little chain of historical notices ;
and further, because it supplies an amusing contrast of
sentiment, as excited by certain exaggerated accounts
of speculatists on the one hand, and actual observation
with the conversation of practical men on the other.
Thus, he was first led by what he had heard to believe,
in his own phraseology, that cotton "mills were places
where young children were, by some inexplicable process, ground — bones, flesh, and blood together — into
yarns and printed calicoes ;" and that the proprietors of
of these mills were "the living representatives of the
ogres and giants of our nursery tales."   Hence it is no
wonder that, when enjoying the hospitality of such men
as Mr. Henry Ashworth of Turton, near Bolton, and

inspecting the admirable economy of the mills and cottages belonging to that gentleman, the ordinary consequences of revulsion of feeling should arise, and that factories and their vicinity should, in the warmth of a kind Irish heart and an excited imagination, become as Eden, and the owners thereof as so many guardian angels. In spite, however, of certain drawbacks on the score of partiality in the favorable estimate of the factory system, much valuable matter occurs in Dr. Taylor's work, exhibiting the folly and the injustice of the monstrous portraitures of mill-work drawn some years ago, the effects of which upon public opinion are as yet far from being extinguished.

SECTION II.

GENERAL FACTS OF THE CASE.

HITHERTO I have endeavoured to maintain, as much as possible, the character of historian, in the observations offered on the sanatory influence of the cotton manufacture. Having now, however, reviewed, though cursorily, the various researches into this matter which have occurred within the last dozen years, as well as examined the contrary views entertained respecting the same, and having thereby obtained a fair amount of data, I shall, in the present section, proceed to offer some remarks upon the whole: and, by the aid of all the facts of the case available to myself, shall present to the reader such general conclusions as I have myself been led to deduce during a residence and practice of some years in the midst of manufactures.

Now, in the first place, I must express my own decided conviction that, in this country at least, the question now before us has, in the various efforts for its elucidation, never been thoroughly divested of extraneous considerations. When the influence of manufactures upon health and life has, at any time, been made the subject of inquiry, it has rarely been discussed and investigated *by itself;* matters bearing upon their general social effects, and questions of political economy, have been so intermingled therewith, that, almost inevitably, the spirit of party has obscured in most cases the perceptions of the investigator, and confused and complicated the entire subject. In what other way can we account for the wonderfully diverse character of the results variously obtained? results too, not affecting a hidden or remote or practically indifferent department of research, nor yet obtained under circumstances allowing with difficulty the customary aids to determine the precise complexion of the related facts ; no, but results that concern the best interests of the community, whose actual condition, upon which the question arises, is observable by all who are anxious for information upon the subject. Whenever such contradictory evidence, as to pure matter of fact, is accumulated, it is a sure sign that the question is more or less beset by prejudice, and involved in the spirit of party. Let the testimony reviewed in the foregoing pages, presented to Mr. Sadler's committee, be again considered. Do we not find an undoubted perversion of fact pervading the whole, with a subtle commitment of eminent medical authorities to the side obviously espoused by the leading members of that committee? How otherwise can we explain the almost universal consent of medical men of undoubted judgment and information, in condemning the manufacturing industry of this country, not as a system complicated with accidental circumstances prejudicial to a sound condition of the human fabric which the improvements which ever follow upon an advancing civilization may be expected progressively to remove, but as one necessarily tending to produce disease, to shorten life, and to destroy population? How, otherwise than by attributing the circumstance to some gross perversion of fact, could the interior of a cotton-mill have been at all compared with that of a chimney choked with soot, as was virtually done by Mr. Morgan in the notable remark before quoted, that "perhaps the employment of a sweep was even worse than these manufactories?" No wonder, indeed, that Dr. Taylor should have been led by this parliamentary evidence to believe that, in factories, young children were ground into yarn and printed calicoes!

I do not myself approach this subject in the spirit which I here condemn, having no conceivable interest in the question, direct or indirect, beyond that which is inspired by a regard for justice, and an anxiety to separate the true from the false; I shall, accordingly, proceed in this discussion in the spirit alike, I trust, of candour and impartiality.

I have said that medical testimony, in sweeping condemnation of the factory system, was obtained through perversion of the facts of the case; let us examine this matter a little more closely. I have before quoted the committee's description of factory labour; and will it, after all the evidence adduced in the foregoing pages, be regarded as faithful? Who that is resident in the manufacturing districts will not be able to confirm Dr. Ure's accuracy, when he states that this labour is not, as maintained, "often continued through the night with scarcely any intervals for recreation or meals?" If the statement have had any foundation in fact at the time it was made, it must have been in some exceptional instance, under special circumstances. The operatives, it is well known, are engaged, as a rule, when in full employment, (much too long, I admit, for the rigid requirements of health), from six in the morning until seven or eight in the evening, with half-hour's pauses for breakfast and tea, and an hour for dinner at home, from twelve to one; and this I imagine to be now almost universal throughout the districts of the cotton manufacture. This is a state of things far from satisfactory as to hygienic conditions, for the young more especially; as it allows, certainly, insufficient periods of repose, in which healthful digestion can take place and out-door exercise be enjoyed. The occupation is not, as averred, necessarily pursued in any unusually " constrained position;" that it is for the most part tedious and monotonous is certain, but this supplies no data for its special condemnation. Let factory labour, in these respects, be compared with many other employments; with those of the tailor, of the dress-maker, &c.; and certainly it will not suffer by the comparison. But the " air is foul and polluted:" let the foregoing extracts from Dr. Ure's work, as to the state of things in Lancashire, and those from M. Villermé as to France, testify to the contrary. Cotton-mills usually are well ventilated. Dr. Cooke Taylor, in the work before referred to, says, " I should be very well contented to have as large a proportion of room and air in my own study as a cotton-spinner in any of the mills of Lancashire." M. Villermé, in treating of this matter, refers to the accusations of unhealthfulness often made against cotton-mills on the score of the employment of oils and certain other greasy materials, which cause disagreeable odours and " pollute" the atmosphere, and thence are considered to operate prejudicially upon the health of those who are subjected to them.

"But," says he, " see these people, interrogate them, interrogate the medical men and other persons who observe the workpeople, and you will very soon be convinced that these things never inconvenience them; that, for the most part indeed, they do not perceive what is so obvious to the senses of strangers; they would, on the contrary, be much more likely to remark their absence, if, by any chance, they should cease all at once. Singular mistakes have arisen in attributing to such causes diseases induced by protracted labour, want of rest, insufficiency of food and its bad quality, habits of improvidence, drunkenness, and, to say all in one word, wages below the actual wants of the recipients."

I wish by no means to constitute myself the apologist of the factory system, as it stands; it is impossible to coincide with Dr. Ure in his excessive eulogies of this labour, as contrasted with rural pursuits; and, assuredly, it ought not to be deemed curative of, or protective from scrofulous disease, as some would appear to maintain. Whilst contending, however, that many of the conditions of health are as little violated by manufacturing industry as by the immense proportion of other pursuits of the working people, I still believe that factory labour is on many accounts injurious; that is to say, when contrasted with the state of the classes raised above that of the operative. How, indeed, can it be otherwise, when regarded as a whole? Individuals thus employed do not spend in the open air more, on an average, than an hour or an hour and a half, in the twenty-four; work is resumed almost the moment the meals are consumed, allowing but little rest for the initiation of a sound digestion; and in the case of the young, there is nearly an entire absence of that delightful " child's play," which the purest feelings of our nature reveal to us as so essential to juvenile health, vivacity, and vigour. Causes like these must and do depress, more or less, the vital energy, and induce, certainly, a lower state of the general health than would exist with the presence of an opposite state of things, as evinced in the pale complexion, the attenuated muscle, the great tendency to what is technically denominated the sub-acute form of disease, and the tedious and uncertain convalescence. But, in all this, we have nothing peculiar to the factory system. With the great majority of the working classes in large towns, the above causes have a general operation. There are the foundries, where machinery is constructed; there are the joiner's shops, the dye-works, the hat manufactories, the tailors' and milliners' workrooms ; there are the letter-press printers' apartments, the compact counting-houses ; indeed, with few exceptions, the conditions of every kind of labour, in any of our modern cities, present almost the same exceptionable points as those of our manufactories, some being more or less favoured in particular respects.

But it may be demanded,—do I believe that no evils occur, specially, to health and life, from the way in which our manufactures are conducted? I must frankly acknowledge, that everything I have either read or seen has led me to the conviction, that diseases, peculiarly attributable to manufactures, are not to be found among the population dependent upon them. And yet the opposite opinion prevails extensively, and has received countenance and support from the express statements of many who have made this subject a matter of investigation. I imagine, however, that preconceived notions have biassed the judgment in these cases, when conclusions have had to be drawn from the facts observed. I suspect that a certain effect has been declared, because, reasoning from analogy, it seemed fairly to be expected. A state of things, calculated to affect a novice in a certain way, does not necessarily produce a similar effect upon the experienced; this wonderfully accommodating principle in the animal economy is too often overlooked in these inquiries; and, hence, it is remarkable how little confirmatory of the anticipation is the actual state of many classes of workpeople. Thus, M. Villermé, in the work before referred to, informs us that he had read a great deal of the insalubrious influence of the woollen manufacture; yet his observations furnish no corroboration of the alleged fact. The late Mr. Thackrah, of Leeds, who was probably the earliest systematic writer in this country on the effects of employments upon health, states, in his excellent work on the subject, that many processes in the woollen manufacture lead to the inhalation of dusty particles, and we have all associated in our minds such a circumstance with protracted irritation in the chest; yet the *sorters* of the wool who are occasionally annoyed with dust from the lime, which in some kinds of wool is used for separating the fleece from the skin, do not, he says, suffer in their health on this account; and, what is yet more remarkable, Mr. Thackrah tells us that the *scourers,* who are all day in a wet room exposed to steam and currents of cold air, are sensible of no ill effects; although, in washing the wool, the workpeople have their arms immersed up to the elbows in warm soap and water, and next carry the article into a room about the temperature of 80° Fahr. to dry, and immediately afterwards, often in a state of perspiration, and always without full clothing, turn out in the open air to fetch more wool; yet, we ever regard such a state of things as directly conducive to pulmonary inflammation and rheumatic affections. Mr. Thackrah, however, distinctly asserts that wool-scourers from these great and frequent transitions are not more subject than others to such diseases ; although, undoubtedly, such an immunity would not have place in parties unaccustomed to such exposure; for habit, in these instances, exerts a vast preservative influence. M. Parent-Duchatelet, in his laborious and standard work on the hygienic condition of Paris, adduces many examples of grievous mistake on the part of speculatists who have attempted to determine *à priori* the actual state of particular classes. There is no question, however, that this law of accommodation operates only within certain limits ; but yet there is such a law, and the extent of its action should be fairly watched and estimated in all such investigations as the present.

I conceive indeed, for my own part, that the great mass of disease constantly witnessed in the districts where manufactures prevail, and so often laid to their account, comes rather from the *great-town* than the *factory* system. The instances just given, to show the futility of mere speculative or analogical reasoning in the decision of such matters, suggest strongly the importance of deducing no inference whatever, except such as shall flow rigorously from the positive facts of the case ; facts numerous in themselves, and selected upon some principle involving neither partiality nor fallacy. Such a proceeding I shall strive to maintain in the attempt to exhibit the accuracy of the position which I have just laid down, that the sanatory ills afflicting large masses of our manufacturing population result from other causes than those to which they have often been attributed.

It must certainly be conceded that a high degree of
civilization is not unattended by some prejudicial circumstances.   Among the more prominent of these in modern
times must be regarded the rapid springing into existence of great towns, which, owing to the circumstances
under which this occurs, arrange themselves in many
cases at utter variance with the requirements of health
on the part of those by whom they are to be inhabited.
The attention of the country is at length being awakened
to this crying evil.   About three years ago a committee
of the House of Commons, after an examination of many
witnesses, reported upon the subject; and if we only
glance at some of the ills revealed, we shall see causes
in operation for the production of disease in towns far
more potent than any that originate essentially with
manufacturing industry. The following passage, amongst
others illustrating the special circumstances prejudicial
to health in the actual state of our large towns, is from
the parliamentary report in question :

" Evidence of the most undoubted credit and of the
most melancholy description has been laid before your
Committee, showing the neglected and imperfect state
of the sewerage, paving, and cleansing in many parts of
London inhabited chiefly by the working classes ; and
similar evidence applies with more or less force to many
other great towns the state of which has been investigated, as Dublin, Glasgow, Liverpool, Manchester,
Leeds, Bradford, &c."

The committee dwell at some length upon the dense
crowding of cellar and other imperfectly-ventilated
residences, as the abundant source of disease in all its
varieties, the ill consequences of which are further
aggravated by the causes enumerated in the extract

just given, occasioning damp, the accumulation of filth, and other well-known springs of disease. It is impossible that causes of this nature can be in constant operation without a terrible deterioration of the health of those who are subject to such noxious agency; and I feel well convinced that here in these things will be found, in combination with destitution and immorality, the effective agents in the production of disease amongst many of those who are engaged in manufactures. Look at the domestic circumstances of the hand-loom weaver, circumstances that have no essential connexion with the nature of his occupation; see the miserable wages, the damp cellar-residences, the small but crowded apartments,—in some cases, several pairs of looms and three or four beds all crammed into what properly constitutes but a moderate-sized room for one bed,—the miserable ventilation and imperfect supply of solar light. This is a state of things falling to the lot of most persons engaged in this, and to that of many also in other occupations, in probably all our modern cities; aye, and in some instances purely from the pernicious influence of habit or example, seeing that many of the working-classes have become so familiarized with this wretched state of things, that when improved wages furnish facilities for emerging from such horrors, there is no scruple in disposing of what to them has become superfluity, in the most disgusting and brutalizing sensuality. It would seem as if familiarity with vice and wretchedness had blunted the sense alike of morality and shame. The whole of this subject has of late, however, received the fullest and most circumstantial investigation from Mr. Chadwick, the secretary to the Poor-Law Commission, whose " Sanatory Report " must ever be regarded as a standing monument of its author's ability, zeal, industry, and public spirit. A mine of information, apparently exhaustless, tending to the elucidation of this subject is discoverable in this remarkable work. Whatever contrariety of sentiment may prevail with respect to the interpretation which Mr. Chadwick has put upon some of his facts, no difference of opinion can exist with regard to the extent of public service which has been rendered by the Report in question.

Amongst other valuable contributions, Mr. Chadwick has collected certain statistical tables which throw a flood of light upon the vexed question forming the subject of the present publication; and these tables I shall in the sequel employ as illustrative of what I have before advanced. They were framed from careful analysis of the death registration books by the clerks of the several poor-law unions, who at the same time act as superintendant registrars. And here, before advancing further, I would submit a few remarks relative to the value of the evidence furnished by our national system of registration; more especially as I propose in the ensuing pages to make very considerable use of the results obtained from this source, not only in determining the average duration of human life in particular localities, but also in attempting to form some approximation to accuracy with respect to the influence of factory employment in the production of diseases especially laid to its account.

The system then of registering every death, in every part of this kingdom, with the age and occupation of the deceased, and with the cause of death so far as practicable, must be allowed by all to constitute a most important auxiliary in the prosecution of all such inquiries as the one in which I am at present engaged, as also in the investigation of certain characteristics of epidemic and contagious diseases. In very minute medical inquiries, or in what is called special pathology, little or no aid can be drawn from this source; but when the object is to determine the *general* character of diseases prevalent in various divisions of the kingdom, or to estimate the agency of many outward causes in the induction of early mortality and fatal diseases at all ages, the facts to be gathered from judicious analysis of the registration books become of the utmost importance. The great defects to be noticed, and those of a character admitting of some correction, consist in the causes of death being generally recorded upon no better authority than the verbal report of parties giving the required information to the registrar,—parties who, unprovided with any medical certificate, furnish their answers, in many cases, in the vaguest and most unmeaning terms, so that a considerable acquaintance with popular phraseology becomes necessary to allow of an *approach* to the real meaning. Yet, in spite of these drawbacks, very satisfactory and practically useful analyses may be made, and the tables planned and obtained by Mr. Chadwick, some of which I am about to exhibit, as well as the highly successful efforts of Mr. Farr in classifying the causes of death, as shown in the appendices to the Registrar-General's Reports, bear witness to the truth of this proposition. The facts arranged and compared are collected upon a principle that applies generally, and are thus exempt from that ordinary source of fallacy in dealing with matters of this kind, the partial selection of uncomparable facts.

In speaking of the sanatory condition of the factory

operatives, I have stated my own belief that, on several accounts, their position was unfavorable to health and longevity ; but that, in this respect, they differed but little, if at all, from other classes of workpeople who were exposed to the same injurious influences, excluding the effects, whatever they be, flowing especially from the factory system; now, Mr. Chadwick's tables show that the value of life at birth is greater in the rural than in the town districts; and that, on the average, the families of professional persons and gentry attain a higher age than do those of tradesmen and farmers; and that these latter again have better chances of life than the working classes. Now these facts are most valuable, as shewing the source of many fallacies that have arisen in the discussion of such questions as the present one; they show that a high average mortality may prevail in a particular locality, not because it is the seat of some special department of industry, but because its labouring population, irrespective of the particular employment, may unduly preponderate. They show that, as a rule, the lower the position of any individual in the social scale, the less favorably situated may he be presumed to be in relation to the conditions of true health; and, upon detailed examination, they show that, as the peculiar evils of the "great-town system" abound, the value of life diminishes accordingly; and, assuredly, Mr. Chadwick's figures do not make an unduly unfavorable exhibition of the towns where manufactures prevail, when contrasted with non-manufacturing towns similarly conditioned in all other respects.

I shall, here, select a few examples, in illustration of what has been just set forth; thus, in the returns of the

average age of death amongst the different classes of
people in manufacturing Manchester and agricultural
Rutlandshire ; the figures stand so :

	Manchester.	Rutlandshire.
Professional persons and gentry, and their families - - - -	38	52
Tradesmen and their families (in Rutlandshire, farmers and graziers are included with shopkeepers)	20	41
Mechanics, labourers, and their families - - - - -	17	38

Now, if in the exhibition of the relative mortality of
the two districts, no account were taken of the different
positions in life of the various classes of the population,
but the low average of life in Manchester set forth in
comparison with what obtains in Rutlandshire, manufactures in all probablity would be referred to as the
cause of such a state of things ; and, indeed, this was
the actual mode of proceeding adopted by Mr. Sadler's
committee; certain returns, very imperfect in themselves, were adduced, and contrasted with others not
for their professed purpose legitimately comparable, because not similarly related with the exclusion of the
factory system to the other possible causes of disease
and early mortality.

The analysed results of our national system of registration have now clearly demonstrated that, in this
country, a densely-populated district is less favorable to
life than one but thinly inhabited ; and the figures just
quoted show that, so far at least as the instance extends,
the result occurs, in a greater or less degree, in all ranks
of life; and thus, in Manchester, where human beings are

densely congregated, influences unfavorable to longevity extensively prevail; for we see that the value of life with the most favoured classes is not greater than with the least favoured in Rutlandshire. If it had appeared that in the higher grades there was little variation in the average age of death in the two localities, the difference in the pursuits of the workpeople in these places might to some extent have confirmed the idea regarding the specially injurious tendencies of manufactures; but the above facts, with many others of a like character, go to show that the evil appertains to *towns* rather than to *factories.*

Bethnal Green, a compact and thickly-populated part of the metropolis, a district where the existing evils of the great-town system, so far as the poor are concerned, prevail to a very great extent, exhibits a highly unfavorable picture of human longevity, especially in the instance of those peculiarly subject to the evils in question. The following applies to Bethnal Green: from a population of 62,018;

	Average Age of Death.
101 Gentlemen and persons engaged in professions, and their families - - - -	45
273 Tradesmen and their families - -	26
1258 Mechanics, servants, and labourers, with their families - - - - -	16

From the above it seems that, whilst in the first and second divisions the chances of life are greater in Bethnal Green than in Manchester, with the third—that representing the working classes—a lower figure is attained. There are yet no factories in this place, the manufactory being chiefly domestic in the department of silk-weaving.

As bearing upon the question relative to the prevalence of disease and death in manufacturing towns, and as tending to decide whether these evils flow essentially from the factories or from other causes, the instances of Manchester and Liverpool seem of all others the most aptly comparable ; they have a somewhat corresponding amount of population, and the towns occupy very nearly the same superficial extent ; the one has been created and lives by the factory system, the other contains, I believe, but one factory, and that of very recent construction, and situated in the suburban locality. The parliamentary report on the health of large towns, in complaining most justly of the sanatory condition of Manchester, observes, however, that " the habitations of the working classes are described as better than those of Liverpool ;" for, as an illustration, it may be stated that, whilst that opprobrium of modern civilization, cellar-residence, extends in the former place only to about 15,000 of the working population, in the latter, so many as 40,000 are subjected to such miserable inhumation in life. Now, the returns of the Registrar-general have ever exhibited a higher rate of mortality, and a presumably greater prevalence of disease in Liverpool than in Manchester, and Mr. Chadwick's analysis displays the following figures :

	Average Age of Death.
137 Gentry and professional persons and their families - - - -	35
1738 Tradesmen and their families - -	22
5597 Labourers, mechanics, servants, and their families - - - -	15

Any one acquainted with the details of our registration system will probably conceive the existence of many inaccuracies in the construction of such tables as the above; and in individual cases, no doubt, some uncertainty must arise in the classification, but not to an extent affecting the general result. Mr. Chadwick, alive to this source of error, caused, in some of his instances, the analysis to be made for several consecutive years, and discovered the strictest uniformity in the issue. Again, out of the many examples afforded in the Sanatory Report, (those I have extracted being merely a few in illustration,) there is the most remarkable coincidence in the inference to which they lead. Hence, I apprehend, that any individual errors arising in the preparation of the tables leaves their *general* accuracy, and consequently their practical value, unaltered.

It is a curious and interesting fact that, in the families of the labouring classes, a greater relative mortality prevails anterior to the age at which factory employment commences than afterwards; this circumstance, Mr. Chadwick has shown in the clearest manner by authentic statistical data, for which I refer to his work.

Do not such facts justify and confirm the opinion which I have before expressed that " the great mass of disease constantly witnessed in the districts where manufactures prevail, and so often laid to their account, comes rather from the *great-town* than the *factory* system?" Do they not suggest that agencies more powerful than manufactures are at work, whose effects, in the language of Dr. Farre applied to factories, go to " diminish population." Mr. Chadwick's work contains certain statements so confirmatory of the present argument that I

again quote from him at some length.   The following is
from page 114 of the Sanatory Report :

" Between different sets of workmen who work at the
same descriptions of work during the same hours, and
in the same town, but in well or ill ventilated factories,
a marked difference in the personal condition and general
health of the workpeople has been perceived. Great
differences are perceptible in the general personal condition of persons working during the same hours in
cotton-mills in towns, and in cotton-mills in rural districts, where they have not only a purer atmosphere, but
commonly larger and more commodious places of abode.
The factory superintendants generally state that the
workers in the country mills are distinguishable at sight
by their more healthy appearance, and by the increased
proportions amongst them who have florid complexions.
Very lately the attention of the Austrian government was
called to the labour of persons in the cotton factories in
the neighbourhood of Vienna. One half, perhaps, of the
mills are of the ordinary construction of the cotton-mills
in England of from thirty to forty years' date, and they
work on an average as much as fifteen hours per diem.
But it appears that the houses in which the workers live
belong to the capitalists who own the mills, many of
whom have displayed a desire to ensure, as far as the
state of the private residences can ensure, the comfort of
those whom they employ, and they have accordingly
built for them a superior description of tenements. It
is stated that the result of the inquiry conducted by the
government physicians was, that the average health enjoyed by the workers in those mills is greater than that
of any other class of workpeople in the neighbourhood

where the mills are situated, and where the general condition of the population is deemed good ; the difference
in the general health of the two classes, (indicated by the
proportions of death, of 1 in 27 of the general population,
and 1 in 31 of the manufacturing population,) was ascribed to the difference of the residences."

I have before maintained, in opposition to Dr. Ure,
that factory labour in towns contrasts very unfavorably
with agricultural pursuits; that, with many other employments, it tends, under present circumstances, to
deteriorate the race, I believe to be undoubted; the
following from the Sanatory Report, at page 185, is
valuable, as illustrating this position :

" In the evidence of recruiting officers, collected under
the Factory Commission of Inquiry, it was shown that
fewer recruits of the proper strength and stature for
military service are obtainable now than heretofore
from Manchester.   I have been informed that of those
labourers now employed in the most important manufactories, whether natives or emigrants to that town, the
sons who are employed at the same work are generally
inferior in stature to their parents. Sir James M'Grigor,
the Director-general of the Army Medical Board, stated
to me the fact, that " a corps levied from the agricultural districts in Wales, or the northern counties of
England, will last longer than one recruited from the
manufacturing towns, from Birmingham, Manchester, or
near the metropolis."   Indeed, so great and permanent
is the deterioration, that out of 613 men enlisted,
almost all of whom came from Birmingham, and five
other neighbouring towns, only 238 were approved for
service."

In connexion with the circumstance recorded in the

above passage, that in Manchester sons have degenerated from their sires, let it be remembered that of late years the sanatory condition of the factories themselves has undergone, questionless, very great improvement. Have not the special disorders of the great-town system gone on, rather, ever increasing? With respect to Birmingham, it will be remembered that it is the seat neither of the cotton, woollen, nor silk manufactures; it is however one of our great towns. It would be tedious to reiterate the obvious inference.

Where is the wonder, after all this, that, in the language of Dr. Bisset Hawkins, "most travellers are struck by the lowness of stature, the leanness, and the paleness which present themselves so commonly to the eye at Manchester?" I feel tolerably certain, however, from a variety of circumstances, that it is only through the medium of spectacles supplied by Mr. Sadler's committee that such a state of matters is observable, "above all amongst the factory classes." Dr. Hawkins, indeed, exhibits throughout the whole of his factory report the strong bias with which he prosecuted his researches as a Commissioner of Inquiry; hence, when in the extract made in the preceding section he says, still speaking of Manchester, "I have never been in any town in Great Britain nor in Europe in which degeneracy of form and colour from the national standard has been so obvious," I much suspect that the obviousness has been *subjective* rather than *objective*. I presume that Dr. Hawkins had visited the worst parts of the metropolis, and had been in Liverpool, Glasgow, and in most other of our large towns.

What shall be said, however, to the *experimentum crucis,* which some may consider Dr. Hawkins's Sunday-school investigation to have constituted ?   In the first place I beg to observe that it is exceedingly difficult to deal with facts such as those which led the factory commissioner to conclude " that the advantage of health is at least double at these institutions on the side of those young people who are not engaged in factories," because we are not informed upon what principle he proceeded in determining the state, as to health, of the respective children in the schools submitted to his examination.   "Good," "middling," and "bad" health cannot be fixed or defined by weight, measure, or numbers ; consequently, the determination of matters in these regards must ever be influenced more or less by the examinant's individual prepossessions, unless he be in ignorance at the time of noting the state of health as to the occupation of the examinand.   Whether this were the case in the particular instance referred to, Dr. Hawkins does not inform us.   Suppose, however, that perfect impartiality prevailed during the entire proceeding, some might explain the unfavorable health predominant among the factory children by adverting to the well-known fact, that Sunday-schools are frequented by many young people whose *homes* are more conducive to good health than are those of the factory children, seeing that the advantages of these institutions are participated in to a considerable extent, often on account of their spiritual rather than their secular benefits, by the classes intermediate between the middle and the lower, as testified by Dr. Hawkins, where he says, "Of the former (inmates of Sunday-schools unconnected with factories), several remain at home and do nothing, some are in service, some are dress-makers, some engaged in the warehouses and shops."   And,

indeed, it is well known to all acquainted with the constitution of Sunday-schools in Manchester, that the
factory members thereof are mostly the worst clad and
least comfortable of all the inmates.   A surer test to
have adopted for deciding upon the relative sanatory
influence of factories would have been, I apprehend, to
take children of the same parents, resident at the same
homes, and to have separated the factory-workers from
those otherwise employed, and thus to have obtained the
numerical results.   Certain facts (amongst others re-
plete with value) somewhat of this character, were
communicated to the statistical section of the British
Association at its meeting in 1842, by Mr. Alderman
Shuttleworth of this town; and these, as applicable
here, I shall extract from the published Report of the
Association's twelfth meeting.   I must not omit the
remarks with which they are prefaced, as herein we
have the guarantee for their accuracy.

"The tables which I have to present to the section
relate to the nineteen cotton-mills in Manchester, which
are engaged in spinning five numbers of yarn . . . . .
it was thought desirable, when the Factory Commission
was appointed in 1833, to collect a body of information
which should be confined exclusively to them as a
separate and distinct class of spinners.   The parties
concerned in the inquiry, anxious to have the facts
collected under such circumstances as to entitle the
statement of them to every degree of confidence, re-
quested me, as a person wholly unconnected with the
spinning business, and having no interested feeling in
the result of the investigation, to undertake the respon-
sibility of conducting it.   I accordingly drew up a series
of questions, to be answered personally and individually

by each operative spinner, to agents, consisting of professional accountants, and one of our most respectable and intelligent surgeons, who were employed to go through the mills and receive the answers from the workmen. That the answers might be given considerately and after due preparation, every spinner was furnished with a list of the questions a day or two before the agents visited them to receive their replies. The facts and statements, thus most carefully and scrupulously collected, were then arranged by me under the heads exhibited in the tables, and afterwards delivered in evidence before the Factory Commissioners sitting in Manchester at the time, and their accuracy verified on oath by myself and the agents employed. . . . . . . The nineteen mills in question worked sixty-nine hours per week; they employed 837 spinners, who are adults. . . . . The married spinners had had 3166 children . . . . 640 of these had worked in cotton-mills, and 58 had worked at other employments. Out of the 640 who had worked in mills, 18, or about $2\frac{3}{4}$ per cent. were dead; and out of the 58 who had worked at other employments, 4, or nearly 7 per cent. were dead."

I draw no positive inference from the above facts; the numbers are too limited to admit of this; but I refer to them as at any rate of greater value than those of Dr. Hawkins, whilst leading to a very different conclusion.

I had the curiosity to repeat the experiment in the instance of St. Augustine's Sunday-school; and, like Dr. Hawkins, selected 50 young persons working in factories, and 50 others either engaged in some different occupation or doing nothing. Their ages ranged from ten to twenty years, and there were about an equal number of each sex. I took the cases entirely at random, just as they fell in my way; and, excepting towards the conclusion of the inquiry, when it became necessary to balance the numbers, I invariably took a note of the state of health prior to making any inquiry as to the occupation. The rule guiding me in the notation of the health was to mark that instance *good* wherein the aspect of the party denoted such a state, and when this received confirmation from the individual's account of his or her actual experience; when the aspect was either delicate, or indicative of the scrofulous taint to any extent, I marked such a case *middling*, even though the person averred that the health had been good; I did the same thing, when the party under examination gave a bad account of the health, though presenting no very obvious traces, outwardly, of such a state of matters; and when the appearance of the individual, and the report supplied, were alike unfavorable, I entered such cases as *bad*. During this investigation, I was most anxious to avoid entertaining any bias with respect to the issue; I felt regardless of what this might be; and, wishful not to anticipate prematurely, I never looked at my notes until the conclusion of the inquiry, which was not until three separate visits had been made to the Sunday-school in question. On arranging the materials, I obtained the following result:

Of the 50 *not in Factories,*
　　　　3 had *bad* health.
　　　19 had *middling* health.
　　　28 had *good* health.
Of the 50 *in Factories,*
　　　　8 had *bad* health.
　　　15 had *middling* health.
　　　27 had *good* health.

Of these 100 instances, 9 resided in cellars ; in every case I recorded my opinion of the health before asking for the residence; I did this that no prepossession might interfere with the impartiality of my notation ; for I have a strong feeling against cellars as places of residence, certainly as strong as any Dr. Hawkins can have had against factories. Of the nine then dwelling under ground, I find, on referring to my notes, that

2 had *bad* health.
5 had *middling* health.
2 had *good* health.

I leave the reader to attach just what value it may seem good to attach to these circumstances ; let them be fairly considered in connexion with all that is gone before ; and I have very little doubt that the conviction will, for the most part, accord with my own, that the low state of health, characterizing so large a portion of our manufacturing population, flows, as I have before said, from the *great-town* rather than the *factory* system.

SECTION III.

ALLEGED PARTICULAR EVILS.

I PROCEED now to examine somewhat more in detail the specific ills alleged to result from the atmosphere of cotton-mills; these being particularly, the premature attainment of womanhood, osseous deformity, consumption, and scrofula. I shall take each of these allegations respectively.

With regard to the first, acceleration of the period of puberty in the female, I am satisfied that considerable mistakes exist; I believe the whole subject to be one upon which many erroneous views prevail. It is an idea almost universally prevalent that maturity in woman occurs regularly at an early or late period of life, according to the high or low temperature of the place of habitation. It is taught systematically, that, with the negress, this condition occurs some years earlier than with most females of the Indo-Germanic race, in consequence of the greater heat of climate to which the former is subjected. This generally received statement, however, there is good reason for believing, rests upon no very satisfactory foundation. On the contrary, my friend Mr. Roberton, in a paper read to the Medical Section of the British Association at its Manchester meeting, brought forward a series of facts well authenticated and promiscuously gathered, which go far to discredit entirely this commonly received statement. It is unnecessary, for my present purpose, to go into any detail of the facts in question; it may be sufficient to assert my own opinion, that Mr. Roberton has clearly shown that the notion respecting the influence of temperature in this matter is at least *not proven;* and, further, that it is probable that the notion is a mere speculation based upon the analogy of what obtains in the vegetable world, having no sure foundation whatever in observation. It is, at any rate, quite certain, that the effect of factories, in this respect, has been inferred from considerations of temperature. Mr. Roberton, with abundant opportunities, from his long residence in this factory metropolis, and with his well-known devotion to statistical pursuits, so far as they relate to physiological conditions, has made this particular matter one of direct investigation; and it has from him received no confirmation of the positive averments of Mr. Sadler's witnesses and others following in their wake, I have myself, again and again, proposed the requisite inquiries for obtaining correct information upon this head, in the full expectation at one time of learning that, with the female inmates of factories, the external indications of maturity occurred much oftener below than above fourteen. Although I have kept no numerical records of the result of such inquiries, I am enabled to state that, in the great majority of cases, this has been in direct opposition to what I formerly anticipated. In one word, I have the fullest conviction, arising from ample experience, that this charge against factories, at any rate, is entirely unfounded.

On the subject of bony distortion among factory work-people, I have already adduced considerable evidence to

discredit the idea that it is so constantly and uniformly
met with as the Report of the Factory Committee would
have led us to believe. I shall again avail myself of
Mr. Shuttleworth's paper, read at the Manchester
meeting of the British Association, because it supplies a
numerical statement upon this subject relating to the
children of persons engaged in the fine spinning-mills,
(usually regarded as the most unfavorable of all to
health,) and themselves also employed in cotton-mills.
"The cases of distortion," says Mr. Shuttleworth, "among
the 640 factory children were 8, or $1\frac{1}{4}$ per cent."   Will
any one contend that this is a very high average? I very
much suspect that a larger proportion would be discovered in grades a little more exalted, especially
amongst young ladies educated at fashionable boarding-
schools.   The precautionary care with which Mr.
Shuttleworth's data were obtained, has been seen from
a previous quotation.   The importance of positive facts
like the above, respecting matters upon which so much
vague declamation had been hazarded, is indeed very
great; they do exhibit certainly, in a very ridiculous
light, the exaggerated statements that went abroad, regarding the terrible influence of factories in the destruction of infant life, and the woful distortions of limb.

Amongst the special ills of the factory system, the
production or premature development of pulmonary consumption, seems to have been more generally dwelt
upon than most of its other prejudicial results.   The
facts and statements of M. Villermé, noticed in the preceding pages, give a peculiar prominence to this presumed consequence of the cotton-manufacture, traceable, in his view of the case, mainly to the bronchial
irritation caused by the inspiration of dust and cotton-

flue, and exhibiting itself in a high degree among the batters and carders, classes of workpeople mainly subjected to this agency. Similar modes of accounting for the assumed result have prevailed also in this country, as will be apparent by a reference to what has been set forth in the early part of this treatise. It will, however, be often noticed that, when in the discussion of any matter of this kind great stress is placed upon the reasons why a certain consequence must follow, there is great cause to distrust the accuracy of the fact itself. Generally speaking, the observer's attention is arrested unduly by instances that seem to realize the expectation, and that which furnishes no corroboration of the anticipation is but little regarded. Medical men, in such cases, too commonly ascribe the results, in the language of Mr. Chadwick, " of a cluster of causes to one ; and in respect to several classes of workpeople, the real cause, the invariable antecedent, is unnoticed." And thus, with minds prepossessed with the notion that tubercular consumption originates essentially in bronchial irritation, and that the atmosphere of cotton-mills is exceedingly conducive to the development of this latter, every case of consumption, occurring among the factory population, is sure to be attributed to the one presumed cause. To obtain any certain and unequivocal information respecting the real state of things is exceedingly difficult, probably impossible ; the facts of the case, to be thoroughly conclusive, must embrace all the particulars of the factory population, so as to be fairly comparable with corresponding facts relating to other classes of persons. Under present circumstances, however, I shall avail myself of the only documents that furnish, impartially, accounts bearing upon this matter, of all sorts of persons in various localities; I refer again to the registers of deaths, in this kingdom, under the superintendence of the Registrar-general. I shall here then examine, in the first place, to what extent these confirm the idea that consumption is more frequent in this manufacturing town of Manchester than in other places; the results I shall compare with corresponding ones gathered from other large towns, where little or no manufacturing prevails; and I shall then subjoin some statistical data obtained by myself from an examination of the registration books of the township of Manchester for a period of three years, data which will contribute, in some degree at least, to satisfy the inquiry as to the proportion which the probable cases of consumption occurring in this place, amongst persons of various pursuits, bear to those happening to the factory population.

The numerical statements which I am about to submit are taken from the third Report of the Registrar-general, the figures applying exclusively to the year 1839: I take this one in preference to the fourth and last because the analyses in the recently-published report, referring to unions in many instances rather than to town districts, do not present figures that allow of the proposed comparison so aptly as the preceding ones; their *relative* import, however, is unaffected whichever of the Reports be appealed to, since on comparing one with another a most remarkable coincidence is witnessed in all the main results, a coincidence which yields one of the strongest proofs of the value of these documents in the prosecution of all researches demanding the aid of statistics. Neither will the circumstance of the decennial census of 1831 being employed for illustration in the third report affect the comparable character of the various places to which allusion may be made, since the subsequent increase of population has been very much in the same proportion in different parts of the country.

According to the census of 1831, there were ascertained to be resident in Manchester and Salford 49,392 families; and the entire deaths registered in 1839 amounted to 9223, of which 1454 are recorded as having been from consumption. This is at the rate of about 3 deaths annually from consumption to every 100 families, and of 15¾ per cent. of the deaths from all causes. This furnishes truly a very decided evidence of the extensive prevalence of the disease in these districts; and taken by itself or compared only with other instances not in all respects rightly comparable, might seem to afford a strong confirmation of the belief that factory employment, so prevalent here, was in a great degree instrumental in the production of this state of things. For, if we take Essex, one of the most purely agricultural counties in the kingdom, we shall discover that with a population of 62,403 families, exceeding by 13,000 the number for Manchester and Salford, the deaths from consumption during the same year were less than in the latter place by upwards of 250; 1201 cases only having been recorded in the death-books of 1839; but the total number of deaths in Essex was also considerably less than with us, in the year in question, there having only been 6352, less by 3000 than those for Manchester and Salford, notwithstanding its larger population. Thus, in Essex, the cases of consumption are not quite 2, annually, for every 100 families. It appears from the above that, in relation to the whole number of deaths from all causes, the cases of consumption were actually fewer in 1839 in this factory district than in agricultural Essex, being in the latter 19 and in the former only 15¾ per cent. Again, if a similar comparison be made with another agricultural division of the kingdom, a similar result will follow; for, in a district embracing Cambridgeshire, Huntingdonshire, and the southern parts of Lincolnshire, comprising a population of 67,351 families, the deaths from all causes were 7306, and those from consumption 1308, or nearly 18 per cent. of the whole; showing, as in the case of Essex, on comparison with these districts, a greatly reduced rate of mortality in general, but not quite a correspondingly low rate from consumption.

In estimating the special condition of Manchester and Salford as to the extent to which consumption prevails, it is best to institute a comparison between these towns and others similarly conditioned, excepting as to manufactures. For this purpose I will take, first, the instance of Liverpool and West Derby, a district, as before expressed, much like our own with regard to its extent, population, and general character of most of the inhabitants, and, not being a manufacturing town, most appropriate of all places, probably, for the present contrast.

In 1831, the census afforded a population of 43,026 families for Liverpool and West Derby, a number 6000 below that for Manchester and Salford, and the deaths altogether for 1839 were 9181, approaching those for Manchester and Salford, during the same year, within 42; and those recorded as from consumption amounted to 1762, or 300 in excess of those with us, notwithstanding our greater population. At this rate, nearly 4 deaths from consumption annually occur in Liverpool for every 100 families, and here only 3; in Liverpool, these cases are little less than 20 per cent. of the deaths from all causes, and in Manchester they are only 15¾. Birmingham, as another large town exempt from factory occupation, may now be drawn into the comparison. According to the census of 1831, 23,932 families resided in that locality; and, in 1839, the registered deaths were 3639. Those from consumption amounted to 668. These numbers furnish a somewhat more favorable evidence of the value of life, and exemption also from consumption, than do those for Manchester, but only to a slight extent; for the proportion exhibited is a fraction below 3 deaths annually, for every 100 families, from the malady in question; while, with us, the number is full 3 per cent. Of the deaths from all causes, about 18 per cent. were from consumption. The metropolis furnishes a smaller number of deaths from consumption, in proportion to its enumerated population, than any of the preceding instances. In 1831, 373,209 families were ascertained to be resident in the metropolitan districts, and the mortality from consumption in 1839, as indicated by that year's registration, reached only 7104 in an aggregate of deaths amounting to 45,441, constituting a rate somewhat below 2 deaths annually, from the disease now under consideration, for every 100 families, and a proportion of deaths from consumption to those from all causes, corresponding exactly with that for Manchester, being somewhat about 15¾ per cent.

These numerical statements, drawn from the national records of the causes of death in various parts of the kingdom, supply certainly no corroboration of the views that have been set forth as to the extraordinary preva-

lence of consumption in the manufacturing districts, as
contrasted with other localities free from manufactories.
Manchester and Salford seem, on the whole, rather more
exempt from the disease than some other places; de-
cidedly more so than Liverpool; but, in comparison with
the agricultural districts and the metropolis, considerably
more subject to its prevalence.   It is a remarkable fact,
however, that, the metropolis excepted, Manchester has
fewer deaths from consumption, in proportion to the
whole number of deaths, than any of the other districts
above instanced; and, contrasted with the metropolis in
this respect, the ratio is the same.   So far we look in
vain for evidence of the baleful influence of the factory
system in developing and causing the increase of the
disease in question.

It might, however, be imagined that, of the deaths
from consumption that did occur in this place, the
factory population furnished an undue proportion.
With a view of ascertaining to what extent this idea
would receive confirmation from the registration records, I was obligingly permitted by Mr. N. Gardiner,
the superintendent-registrar of this district, to deduce
such particulars from the documents in question as
seemed fitted for throwing light upon this matter.
Conceiving that a period of three years would yield a
fair average result, I selected the death-books of the
township of Manchester for the years 1838-39, and 40,
and took therefrom the age and stated occupation of all
persons registered as deceased from " consumption,"
" decline," and " phthisis," between the ages of fifteen
and forty, admitting those that had attained the former
age, and rejecting such as were not below forty.   My
view in the detail of this proceeding was, that as

Manchester—to the exclusion of the out-districts, so
called, of this union, and of Ardwick, Chorlton-upon-
Medlock, Hulme, and Salford—contains, at least, its fair
share of the factory population here, it would also, for
my present purpose, afford a tolerably just type of the
remainder of the population—of that not dwelling
within what constitutes the actual township. I have,
for several reasons, confined my choice of instances to
those deceased between the ages of fifteen and forty;
in the first place, because it is reasonable to suppose
that, if occupation of any kind operate very materially
so as to shorten life, through the production of such a disease as consumption, the affection will be developed and
terminate fatally within those periods. And, again, I
considered that, in omitting, for the purposes of this inquiry, the instances marked consumption, decline, or
phthisis, when under fifteen and above forty, I should
be most likely to embrace the largest average of real
cases, seeing that, in the records of the causes of death,
infants of the tenderest age, even those below twelve
months, are very frequently registered as having died
from decline or consumption: and, on the other hand,
persons of very advanced years are often similarly
registered; there being a high probability that, in both
these extremes, a large proportion of the cases thus
registered have not been really of consumption, but, in
the case of children, probably some mesenteric affection,
and in that of persons past middle life, most likely
chronic bronchitis or general decay from old age. Not
that I feel any confidence of having obtained by the
present plan cases only of true consumption, for many
deaths from other organic affections, especially of the
abdominal viscera, are in all probability registered on

the imperfect report of those supplying the required information, as " decline," and others, real consumption, are very likely given in as " disease of the chest" or " weakness ;" still, on the whole, I dare say that, as regards *numbers* a very fair accuracy will be gained, the cases improperly included being balanced by those unduly excluded.

The township of Manchester, then, with a population of about 160,000, and with an annual average of deaths amounting to 6000, afforded 1141 registered deaths from consumption, within the above-stated ages, during the three years before mentioned ; and 377 of these do not appear to have followed any definite pursuit, being described for the most part as *wives, daughters*, or *sons*, not connected with any business ; in the remaining 754, the employment was stated, though often in phraseology somewhat ambiguous.* The following constitutes the result of an analysis ; the terms below being given very much as they occur in the registration books.

Registered Occupation of Deceased.	Number Registered.	Registered Occupation of Deceased.	Number Registered.
Auctioneer - -	1	Brush-maker - -	3
Agent - -	3	Bricklayer -	4
Bookkeeper - -	15	Bonnet-maker -	2
Baker - -	2	Boatman - -	3
Brewer - -	6	Bookseller - -	1
Butcher - -	6	Boiler-maker -	2
Bust-maker - -	1	Batter - -	2
Brace-maker -	1	Barrister - -	1

* The Registrar-general has recently made great exertions to procure more exactness in the registration of the causes of death. Would not this laudable proceeding be well followed up by corresponding efforts to obtain greater precision in the records of the occupations of the deceased?

Registered Occupation of Deceased.	Number Registered.	Registered Occupation of Deceased.	Number Registered.
Comb-maker	1	Fustian-cutter	12
Clogger	1	Frame-tender	11
Charwoman	4	Fishmonger	2
Chair-maker	1	Furrier	1
Carder	11	Fruiterer	1
Clerk	2	Grinder	1
Chandler	1	Glazier	2
Callenderer	2	Glass-worker	4
Cooper	1	Green-grocer	1
Coal-merchant	1	Gas-fitter	1
Cutter	1	Groom	1
Coachman	6	Hardware-dealer	1
Cap-maker	2	Hatter	11
Carter	2	Hawker	5
Currier	2	Hair-dresser	4
Clothes-dealer	1	Horse-dealer	2
Carver	1	Joiner	19
Collier	2	Iron-founder	1
Coach-proprietor	1	Japanner	1
Draper	1	Knitter	2
Dress-maker	10	Lodge-keeper	1
Dyer	12	Liverystable-keeper	1
Doubler	5	Labourer	45
Dresser	10	Leather-dresser	1
Doffer	1	Medical man	3
Druggist	1	Millwright	5
Engineer	7	Miller	2
Engraver	3	Mechanic	21
Eatinghouse-keeper	1	Maker-up	5
File-cutter	1	Milk-dealer	1
Factory-worker (particular employment not stated)	10	Milliner	4
		Musician	3
		Moulder	3

Registered Occupation of Deceased.	Number Registered.	Registered Occupation of Deceased	Number Registered.
Minister	1	Sawyer	4
Match-maker	1	Solicitor	1
Manufacturer	1	Shop-keeper	3
Overlooker	5	Silk-worker	2
Paper-maker	1	Sizer	1
Painter	6	Seaman	1
Piecer	28	Stationer	1
Porter	11	Slater	1
Picker	1	Sail-maker	1
Pawnbroker	1	Soldier	1
Pedlar	2	Stripper	3
Plasterer	2	Stock-maker	1
Post-boy	1	Skinner	1
Printer	9	Striker	1
Policeman	2	Traveller	4
Paper-stainer	1	Tea-dealer	1
Packing-case-maker	2	Tailor	20
Pattern-maker	2	Timber-merchant	1
Packer	4	Turner	1
Pressman	1	Tobacconist	2
Ruler	1	Twister-in	1
Reeler	15	Tinplate-worker	1
Reed-maker	2	Umbrella-maker	2
Rope-maker	1	Warehouse man	4
Roller-coverer	1	Weaver	102
Stay-maker	1	Winder	29
Stretcher	3	Warper	3
Shoe-maker	23	Waiter	3
Spinner	45	Wine-merchant	2
Stone-mason	8	Wire-worker	2
Servant	33		
Smith	8	Total	764
Spindle-maker	5		

Now, in order to effect the complete solution of the problem, whether or not the deaths from consumption in Manchester preponderate among the factory population, much more extensive and precise data are required than any which the above table supplies. The number of persons, with their respective ages, engaged in each department of business, would need to be ascertained, as well as the relative mortality from all causes prevalent in the different classes of workpeople; and, above all, in any attempts to ascertain facts of this kind, there is absolute need that precision in the use of terms should be observed. Inquiries of this nature, however, cannot, on many accounts, be prosecuted by individuals.* In the absence, however, of data for coming to a positive determination upon this subject, I will strive to make the most of the materials that exist, and hope, in this way, to form some reasonable approximation to the real state of the case.

In reviewing the terms descriptive of the occupation of the deceased, we can have but little doubt that the following refer to factory employment: batter, carder, doubler, doffer, factory-worker, frame-tender, overlooker, piecer, picker, stretcher, spinner, silk-worker, stripper, warper. If so, by referring to the table, it will be found that a total of 130 becomes thus obtained. The terms dresser, reeler, weaver, and winder are ambiguous. The hand-loom weavers work at their homes, but those engaged with power-looms are in factories; any attempt to discriminate between the two classes of weavers, by aid

---

* Might not the value and importance of the Manchester Statistical Society's labours be greatly enhanced by researches in this direction? Their resources are known to be ample.

of the registration records, would have been vain ; in these documents, the expression, though occasionally distinctive enough, is so frequently " weaver" simply, that no successful division could have been made ; hence, whenever the terms power-loom weaver, steam-loom weaver, silk-weaver, hand-loom weaver, or merely weaver, occurred in the progress of my analysis, all were placed in the same category. There are "winders," within, and without, factory walls. The same remark applies to the term reeler. Dresser is a term indicating factory employment, but there are dressers also connected with the dyeing business. Now, speaking from the imperfect knowledge which I have of these matters, I should suppose that about two thirds of the deaths among weavers from consumption, as furnished in the above table, refer to the hand, and the remaining third to the power-loom class ; that, of winders the great proportion, say three fourths, would in all probability be engaged at their homes, or in warehouses, rather than in factories ; that of reelers, about one fourth may be excluded from the ranks of the operatives in cotton-mills ; and of dressers, that possibly equal numbers may have been in, and out of, factories. This estimate is not formed arbitrarily, but after some consideration, aided by conversation with practical men ; hence, if correct, we shall notice a total of 187 deaths in three years, from consumption in the township of Manchester, between the ages of 15 and 40, amongst the factory population, of 577 with persons of various other pursuits ; and of 377 happening to those without any probable employment, in the way of a business. Thus the deaths amongst the factory people would stand as follows :

Batters	-	-	-	2
Carders	-	-	11
Doublers	-	-	5
Doffer	-	-	-	1
Dressers	-	-	-	5
Employment not stated	10
Frame-tenders	-	11
Overlookers	-	-	5
Piecers	-	-	-	28
Picker	-	-	-	1

Reelers	-	-	-	11
Stretchers	-	-	3
Spinners	-	-	45
Silk-workers	-	-	2
Strippers	-	-	3
Winders	-	-	7
Warpers	-	-	3
Weavers	-	-	34
Total	-	187

Now, it may be proper to state here, what is well known to those having local acquaintance with Manchester, that the township is inhabited most disproportionately by the working classes. Excepting medical men, and second-rate shopkeepers, and publicans, it is almost the constant rule, even with those whose places of business are central, to reside either in the suburbs, or in the townships of Ardwick, or Chorlton-upon-Medlock; places which, within what is commonly regarded and designated as the town of Manchester, only *border* upon the actual *township*, being generally selected for residence, by those whose resources will admit of such a proceeding, from considerations of health. Under such circumstances, where there is only conjecture to guide, it may not be very hazardous to assume that not very much less than one sixth of the inhabitants of Manchester township, between 15 and 40 years of age, are employed in factories ; and, if so, no corroboration is afforded, by the death registers, of the notion that consumption is disproportionately prevalent among the factory population, seeing that 187 in 1141 constitutes a ratio to correspond. Any error, which may have arisen

in the estimate, is open to correction ; for which purpose
I have introduced at length, the tabular list upon which
the calculations rest.

It has often been supposed, and in the notable parliamentary evidence in 1832 it was stated again and
again, that factory labour prematurely exhausts the vital
energy, and gives rise to an unusually early mortality
from various diseases of a slow, chronic character.
Assuredly, if such were the fact, it would be obvious in
the mortality manifested by the fatal cases registered as
" decline ;" and the instances of consumption occurring
in such a place as Manchester would, if not more numerous than elsewhere, at least invade and destroy the
population at an earlier period of life.   The best table,
because the most promiscuous in its materials and extensive in its basis, which I remember to have seen,
illustrating the age at which consumption carries off its
victims, is that supplied by Sir James Clark, in his
admirable work on tubercular phthisis.   It shows the
proportion, at different ages above fifteen, of 1000 deaths
from the malady under discussion, and it is deduced from
an average of observations made in Edinburgh, Berlin,
Nottingham, Philadelphia, Chester, Carlisle, and Paris ;
I abstract the following from the table in question,
exhibiting the relative numbers dying between fifteen
and forty :

Aged.		Number of Deaths.
15 and under 20	- - -	99
20 „ 30	- - -	285
30 „ 40	- - -	248

These figures bear substantially the same relation to

each other as those which prevail in manufacturing Manchester; for, anxious to see what confirmation of the idea respecting the early invasion of consumption in the factory districts would arise from the registration books, I classified the ages of the 1141 according to periods of five years, and obtained the following result:

Aged.								Deaths.
15 and under 20	-		-		-		-	195
20	„	25	-		-		-	- 243
25	„	30	-		-		-	- 260
30	„	35	-		-		-	- 223
35	„	40	-		-		-	- 220

Total 1141

If, from the returns upon which Sir James Clark's table is based, we take an illustration from separate series of cases whose aggregate amount approaches the numbers just analyzed, we shall obtain figures almost exactly corresponding with those supplied by my own analysis. Thus, by including only certain tables referring to Carlisle and Paris, a total will be gained of 1155, those for Manchester being 1141; the numbers, at various ages, of the respective series, stand as under:

Aged.					Carlisle and Paris.			Manchester.
15 and under 20	-		-		196	-	-	195
20	„	30	-	-	515	-	-	503
30	„	40	-		- 444	-	-	443

Total 1155   1141

These figures present a most remarkable accordance in the ages of persons dying of consumption under very different external circumstances ; and, at the same time, from the fact of this accordance, enhance the value of the evidence afforded by a selection of cases from the registration books, as true consumption, on the principle of recognizing as such those, and those only, entered as decline, consumption, and phthisis; and, from such evidence, all foundation seems to be wanting to the idea that the population of Manchester, as the best type of a factory district, is at all more liable to *early* invasion of consumption, than that in other places.

The above facts show satisfactorily, in the judgment of the present writer, that, whatever may occur in France, where probably certain other conditions of health may be less favorable than in this country, the factory system does not lead *necessarily* to the undue prevalence of consumption.   In no place do cotton-mills abound so extensively as in Manchester, leading to the presumption that if there be anywhere, as mentioned by M. Villermé, a " cotton-phthisis," it is an accidental and not an essential appendage.

The abundance of scrofula, in all its varieties, has very generally been dwelt upon, as characterizing a manufacturing population ; and this was most commonly ascribed by the medical and other witnesses before the parliamentary committee to the direct influence of the factory system, as I have sufficiently illustrated in the early part of this publication.   Now, it is exceedingly difficult to grapple with allegations of this kind.   Scrofula constituting rather a speciality in the habit of body modifying disease than a specific disease itself, how shall its presence in many cases be assured ?   The scrofulous taint may be so palpable and obvious that no mistake whatever in some given instance could possibly arise.

There are other habits of body of so healthful and vigorous a character that any moderately competent judge would in a moment declare them to be free from every vice of the kind. These, however, form the extremes; the intermediate cases are by far the most numerous, and there are some examples of so doubtful a character that two physicians of equal ability and experience should probably differ with respect to the presence or absence of what is called the scrofulous taint. Under such circumstances it is no wonder that many medical men should speak of the abundance or scarcity of scrofula, rather from anterior prepossession, than from a patient and analytical investigation of the real facts of the case, there being so little of the positive about this matter to fix the standard. Look at the contradictory assertions as to this matter noticed in the preceding pages. Go back to the oracular averment of the late Dr. Carbutt, that, from his own experience, scrofula is almost unknown in cotton mills; and that, when present, it is cured by them rather than aggravated! Contrast this with the stated results of Mr. Malyn's experience, in the same field of observation, at a period somewhere contemporary, to the effect that scrofula was ten times more prevalent in Manchester than he had ever witnessed it to be in any other place, and that he had been led to ascribe all this to the factories! Assuredly, I shall not risk a similar error, by adducing any *general* experience of my own, vague and unrecorded; I can, however, easily understand, how Mr. Malyn saw an immeasurably larger number of cases of scrofula in Manchester than during his subsequent metropolitan career, as stated in his evidence before parliament. In Manchester, he tells us that, as physician's clerk to the

Infirmary, his business was solely with the most destitute classes; it is reasonable to suppose that his professional pursuits, after engaging in private practice,
were of a somewhat different character in London, bringing him at any rate into communication less frequently
with the lowest social grades; on which account, he
would not be so likely to encounter scrofulous disease as
under his former circumstances.   In all investigations
of this kind, however, little value can be attached to the
results of partial observation, even when accurate; or to
any aggregate of facts, which have not been obtained
generally and promiscuously.

M. Villermé, in the work before mentioned, remarks
upon the extensive prevalence of scrofula among the
body of operatives in the manufacturing towns of
France; but he sufficiently explains the cause, when he
sets forth, how this scourge, in all its hideous varieties,
afflicts the inhabitants of great towns, especially the
poor, accumulated in narrow streets, in filthy, dark, and
ill-ventilated lodging-houses, places but rarely perme-
ated by the solar ray.   "But," he states, "manufactures,
even in their actual organization, must not be blamed
exclusively for this state of things; the evil is not
peculiar to them; it was assuredly not less frequent formerly, in proportion to the existence of other insalubrious
conditions, when the present manufacturing system had
not sprung into existence."   M. Villermé says that it is
chiefly in a mediate, in an indirect manner, that most of
these evils arise; the kind of food, the clothing and
lodging, the degree of fatigue, the continuance of the
hours of labour, and the moral conduct of individuals,
are the main circumstances which influence the health
prejudicially or otherwise; and, with a beneficial cha-

racter of these conditions, many of the accidental causes of disease would lose their efficacy.

In reflecting upon the precise value to be attached to the records of consumption obtained by our national system of registration, it occurred to me that probably they might furnish some clue to the relative prevalence of scrofula in various localities, seeing that consumption is not only a scrofulous disease (according to preponderance of authority) in itself, but the mode in which other scrofulous affections often terminate fatally; thus, scrofula, affecting the spinal column, or any of the joints, generally ends in pulmonary consumption in the event of a fatal issue. Moreover, some little acquaintance with popular modes of dealing with these matters satisfies myself that the cases of death, in many instances, reported to the registrar as *decline* or *consumption*, are representative of general scrofulous disease rather than of phthisis exclusively. A consumption or decline, with the mass of the lower orders, is expressive of most diseases unaccompanied by acute symptoms, and marked by progressive emaciation; and I very much think that, where the scrofulous taint prevails extensively, the cases of death registered as decline and consumption will on this account be in excess. Hence, I apprehend it to be somewhat presumable that in those places where, of the whole number of deaths registered, the proportion of consumption cases is great, the existence of much scrofula may be inferred. Of course, I only propose this scheme as one furnishing, probably, an *approximation* to the actual fact.

To apply this scheme, I will take the several towns, analysed with respect to these matters, as they occur in the Report of the Registrar-general, of which I have made such ample use in the foregoing pages. Thus, in the exceedingly mixed population of the metropolis, out of 45,441 deaths, 7104 were registered as from consumption, being in the proportion of 1 in $6\frac{1}{3}$ in the cotton districts of Manchester and Salford, 9223 deaths furnished 1454 cases of consumption, being in the same proportion as in the metropolis ; in commercial Liverpool, all but exempt from manufactures of any kind, 9181 deaths gave 1762 instances of consumption, or 1 in $5\frac{1}{3}$; in the case of Leeds, the seat of the woollen manufacture, a total of 4388 yielded 804 of consumption, or 1 in $5\frac{1}{2}$; and in Birmingham, where there are no cotton-mills, 3639 deaths included 668 cases of consumption, or 1 in every $5\frac{1}{2}$.   So it would appear that Manchester, with its factories, exhibits in its fatal cases of disease a somewhat moderate proportion of those here presumed to be of a scrofulous character.   Just then to the extent that the test here applied may be considered to possess any value, it tends to disprove the notion regarding the extraordinary prevalence of scrofula in the districts of the cotton manufacture.

In bringing this treatise to a close, I think myself in some degree entitled, from all that has preceded, to conclude that no peculiar evils attach necessarily to manufacturing pursuits. That the position of the labouring classes as a whole is comparatively prejudicial in these respects, I conceive to be pretty well made out ; and this more particularly in the case of such as inhabit the ill-conditioned localities in our large towns ; and in so far as factories and other corresponding places of labour interfere with the right conditions of health, they of course lead to the production of disease and the shortening of life. I think, however, that upon a review of the facts and circumstances discussed in the preceding pages, the evils afflicting the working-classes in this point of view will be considered to appertain to their *domestic* rather than to their *industrial* relations ; and yet badly as I regard the hygienic state of many of our modern cities, it is yet impossible to go the lengths of Sir A. Carlisle in his parliamentary evidence, in concluding that because *he* could not find a person of the fourth generation by both the father and mother's side in the city of London, therefore our towns would undergo depopulation in a comparatively brief space of time, if not refreshed by accessions from the country. When the migratory character of our town populations is considered, I do not think Sir A. Carlisle's fact—the experience of a single inquirer—very extraordinary ; and assuredly it warrants no such conclusion as the one which he seems to have deduced. Great evils undoubtedly follow in the train of advancing civilization ; but, in the phraseology with which I set out, these must be regarded not as something inseparable from such a state of things, but as the result of that imperfection of humanity which in no instance can anticipate, with a view to provide for, every possible consequence of social changes, allowing man to become enlightened not in all things at once but only progressively. In admitting most fully the evils of our present state of society, I cannot reprobate too much the folly of those who would fasten upon isolated points and expend their humanity and energy in decrying special departments of industry, rather than, with a more general philanthropy and with a sounder judgment, in probing the real source of the attendant evil, so as to ascertain how its removal can be effected without the infliction of greater evils upon the community at large. When from party-spirit, or from excited imagination, or from eccentric modes of looking at particular subjects, statements are hazarded to the effect that, as before quoted, " in English factories everything which is valuable in manhood is sacrificed to an inferior advantage in childhood. You purchase your advantage at the price of infanticide; the profit thus gained is death to the child :" or, when a depopulation of cities in fifty years is proclaimed to be the natural consequence of their existing ills; the investigation of the real question is prejudiced; and men, revolting from the exaggeration, too readily shut out the prospect of the real evil, and deny its existence. It is much better to regard the entire subject from a more general point of view, and to discuss the sanatory condition of our working population as a whole; for, assuredly, it needs vast and ample improvement; and, here, there is scope for the widest and most comprehensive philanthropy. Let efforts be made to obtain a check to the way in which the present residences for the poor are constructed; let considerations respecting the health of the future inmates of these places, over and above those which flow from motives of cupidity, be required imperatively to preside in the control of these matters; let the dwellings of the humblest of our fellow-creatures be preserved, as much as possible, from miasm and pollution—the sources of disease and death—by appropriate drainage and sewerage under-ground, by just supplies of pure air from above and around, and by a certain enforced cleanliness within. Above all, in any future enactments in this direction, let cellars, as places of human habitation, be repressed, if not progres-

sively extinguished, which latter proceeding would
constitute a great boon to humanity. In this way,
might the health and the strength of the productive
classes to a considerable extent be maintained, and the
race invigorated. Notwithstanding the prodigious sums
of money appropriated to the treatment of the sick poor,
I hesitate not to affirm that the present system requires
considerable alteration. The application, upon a more
extensive scale, of the *hospital* to the discouragement of
the present *dispensary* system, is a great desideratum ;
nine tenths of the cases of disease, occurring amongst
the destitute classes in large towns, demand, most imperatively, *good nursing* for their cure, and very little
physic ; whereas, under existing circumstances, the
required state of things is reversed, and large numbers
get little or no nursing in sickness, but excess of physic.
I broach no medical heresy here ; what I now say is
common conversation amongst all instructed members of
the profession, but here is not the place to go into any
detail upon this subject. In dealing, however, with the
sanatory state of the labouring population, it is well to
regard the matter not in one merely, but in the whole
of its phases. In this way, all irritating topics may be
avoided, and an effective effort be calculated upon with
a view to provide the appropriate remedies for the
removable ills that do actually exist.

C. AND J. ADLARD, PRINTERS, BARTHOLOMEW CLOSE.